CW00519760

Jo Ellis grew up in Suffolk and is currently still living there. Jo has had many jobs in retail before attending university as a mature student doing a three-year BA (degree). She is now working as a writer.

For my children, Kelan and Daisy.

Jo Ellis

DANGER, DARKNESS AND DESTITUTION IN NINETEENTH CENTURY BRITAIN

AUSTIN MACAULEY PUBLISHERS™

LONDON • CAMBRIDGE • NEW YORK • SHARJAH

Copyright © Jo Ellis (2021)

The right of Jo Ellis to be identified as author of this work has been asserted by the author in accordance with section 77 and 78 of the Copyright, Designs and Patents Act 1988.

All rights reserved. No part of this publication may be reproduced, stored in a retrieval system, or transmitted in any form or by any means, electronic, mechanical, photocopying, recording, or otherwise, without the prior permission of the publishers.

Any person who commits any unauthorised act in relation to this publication may be liable to criminal prosecution and civil claims for damages.

A CIP catalogue record for this title is available from the British Library.

ISBN 9781528929271 (Paperback)
ISBN 9781528965811 (ePub e-book)

www.austinmacauley.com

First Published (2021)
Austin Macauley Publishers Ltd
25 Canada Square
Canary Wharf
London
E14 5LQ

Introduction

It has now been seventeen years since Alison Rattle and Allison Vale published the story of Amelia Dyer; a woman who murdered babies for money. Dyer was arguably the most prolific British baby-farmer of the nineteenth century. Rattle and Vale brought to light the horrific trade known as baby-farming, this opened many doors for historians to delve into the forgotten world of Victorian female criminals. I will examine Dyer's crimes, which led to one of the most shocking trials of the nineteenth century. The event shone a spotlight on the Victorian crime of 'baby-farming'. I will seek to investigate what had made this seemingly respectable woman descend to such cruelty. Serial killers are made and not born, with a dysfunctional memory or warped feeling of low self-esteem, usually from an early age a seed had been planted.

However, there is an ongoing debate of 'nature versus nurture'. Was Dyers crime caused by factors in her biological make-up, or were they a consequence of some unknown trauma in childhood or social and economic circumstances?[1]

---

[1] Dr Peter Joyce, *Criminology, A complete introduction.* (Great Britain, Hodder & Stoughton.2012), p. 34.

A sociological approach focuses on the awareness in which a negative social sphere can manipulate someone's actions, such as poverty, unemployment and deprivation.[2]

The word 'serial killer' brings forth vivid images to many people, horrific distress and oppression. Dyer seemingly committed these horrifying acts without appearing to have any guilt or remorse. The devastation of her actions towards vulnerable women, was her true pleasure in life. This woman was what we now know as a 'psychopath'. Haunting the imagination of those who study her, the ability to murder infants for profit without any remorse, Dyer, dominated the headlines in late Victorian England. Serial murder excites the public imagination, and no details of the grisly murders were omitted. Social conditions within Victorian England enabled Dyer to get away with organising her grim business for allegedly over twenty-years. High infant mortality rates were a sad fact in the nineteenth century, and early deaths were often overlooked by the authorities. Like most serial killers a tabloid name was given to them, in this instance Dyer was commercially known as 'the angel maker'. Dyer's 'work' is murder, so by giving her a nickname, she was popularised. With a connection between her nickname and real name is unfortunately lost, feeding into our nature, everything must be labelled. Women who kill are generally labelled 'mad, sad or bad'. My dissertation focus will be about Amelia Dyer, and baby-farming in mid to late Victorian England. I will also focus on themes surrounding the crime, including a brief overview towards female offenders and the circumstances surrounding their crimes.

---

[2] Dr. Peter Joyce, *Criminology,* p. 35.

Amelia Dyer came to the attention of the public after she committed the most heinous of crimes. As she became known as 'the angel of death', she was inevitably sentenced to death by hanging at Newgate Prison on 10 June, 1896. Although it is believed that she was responsible for the death of anywhere up to four hundred infants, she was convicted solely for the murder of an infant named Helena Fry. Her body was found in the Thames at Reading in 1896, helping secure the conviction of Dyer. My research will demonstrate how criminal woman challenged the stereotype of them as being passive, frail, subservient and ultimately dependant on men. It will bring to light how notorious women refused to accept their place in a male society. I will not concentrate in too much detail on women and gender itself, but this will be an important angle about this type of extraordinary crime, and the difference between men and woman and how class divisions mattered. There is little known about Dyer's early years, certainly nothing that would raise any alarm bells to indicate why she committed these depraved acts. In fact, Dyer was considered as extremely lucky, all things considered. Her parents valued education and her father was a well-respected, hard-working man as a master shoemaker.[3] Dyer was born in 1838, in the city of Bristol. Less than ten years previously, there was an outbreak of cholera that swept across the city, this was known as the 'great panic' and was reported in *The*

---

[3] Alison Rattle and Allison Vale, *The Woman Who Murdered Babies for Money, The Story of Amelia Dyer.* (London, Carlton publishing group 2011), p. 28.

Times.[4] Bristol like many other cities were marked with slums; entire families lived in rooms where space was limited, dark, damp and riddled with parasitic crawlies and the dregs of society. Disease and misery were trademarks of daily life and crime was widespread. While Dyer had escaped most misery, she was haunted by the final days of her mother's death. Only in her 40s, she had caught typhus fever. Dyer witnessed her mother's health rapidly decline, witnessing symptoms such as delusions, and hallucinations. This finally transcended to meningitis and inevitably brought forth a swift death.[5] Piecing together this dark story of mayhem and madness, the sinister trade of Victorian baby-farming. The case of Amelia Dyer led to the creation of modern child protection laws. One hundred and twenty-two years later, I aim to draw attention to one of Britain's most disturbing serial killers.

Rattle and Vale point out that the system was inadequate in safeguarding child welfare, and that the authorities were ill-equipped to take on this task.

Therefore, they state, many babies and children died in baby farms, where the fee for their care was the only thing that mattered, and once that had been received, the babies, "were often starved or drugged to death; some met a speedier

---

[4] Anthony S. Wohl, *Endangered Lives, Public Health in Victorian Britain.* (Cambridge, Cambridge University press, 1983), p. 119.
[5] Alison Rattle and Allison Vale, *The Woman Who Murdered Babies for Money, The Story of Amelia Dyer.* (London, Carlton publishing group 2011), pp. 28-29.

end and were murdered outright,"[6] states Vale. Additionally, Vale states, "Dyer was finally tried for her crimes and executed in 1896 at Newgate, for the murder of 300 babies."[7] "Baby farming is to an extent ignored or forgotten today," according to Vale, "except in the realm of true crime."[8] In an article in *The Independent*, Allison Vale accounts for the contemporary rise of interest in the topic: "While largely forgotten today, Amelia Dyer's crimes paved the way for one of the most sensational trials of the Victorian era – and spotlighted the pandemic problem of infanticide in nineteenth-century Britain."[9] Among true crime authors, interest has grown in Amelia Dyer as an example of a notorious baby farmer, as can be seen from the number of sources referred to in this article as part of my contextual study of Rattle and Vale's *The Woman Who Murdered Babies for Money: The Story of Amelia Dyer.*

---

[6] Alison Rattle and Allison Vale, *the woman who murdered Babies for Money, The Story of Amelia Dyer.* (London, Carlton publishing group 2011), p. 13.

[7] Alison Vale, *"Amelia Dyer: The Woman Who Murdered 300 Babies" The Independent*. Friday 22 February 2013. As seen on 09/04/2018.

[8] Vale, *"Amelia Dyer: The Woman Who Murdered 300 Babies" The Independent*. Friday 22 February 2013. As seen on 09/04/2018.

[9] Vale, *"Amelia Dyer: The Woman Who Murdered 300 Babies" The Independent*. Friday 22 February 2013. As seen on 09/04/2018.

Chapter One
The Beginning of the End

On the bitterly cold morning of Monday, March 30th, 1896, a local man, Charles Humphreys, a boatman, was going about his usual routine of navigating the River Thames near Reading.[10] This was nothing unusual for the busy waterway traffic of barges and smaller vessels, transporting goods in a thriving area of docklands. Underneath a wooden footbridge, Humphreys pulled his barge close to something that has caught his eye stuck in the tall river reeds, a brown paper package bobbing up and down on the river. Humphreys pulled out the damp package dragging it through the water onto his boat. The half-sodden parcel was lumpy and heavy. Humphreys unwrapped the package, expecting to find goods or something of value; however, beneath the paper was a fabric of flannel, once pulled aside, this exposed to his horror, as described in the Berkshire news, "In the parcel was the body of a baby girl; she had been strangled with white tape that had been tied twice around her neck and knotted under her left ear. The police would soon find that her horrific

---

[10] Angela Buckley, *Amelia Dyer and the Baby Farm Murders*.
(Reading, Manor Vale Associates, 2016), p. 1.

injuries would form a sinister pattern."[11] Similarly, in the *Berkshire Chronicle*, "There can be little doubt that the police have unearthed a case which will prove the most remarkable in the annals of crime for many years past."[12] *History by the Yard* wrote, "One of the more distasteful aspects of Victorian England was the practice of taking in unwanted babies, and, in return for a commercial fee, either over-crowding them or killing them. It was known as baby farming."[13] Humphreys' discovery of the infant was the beginning of the end for Amelia Dyer. What could have led a woman to have committed such an unspeakable crime?

The discovery of the infant's body strangled and subsequently dumped in the Thames was the beginning of the end for Dyer. Detective Constable Anderson was first to investigate the parcel unearthed by Charles Humphreys. After close inspection, the officer could see faint writing on the parcel, as the package was stuck amongst the reeds it did not sink enough to wash away all the address. Anderson investigated the parcel address, after carefully examining the paper that had been wrapped around the infant. It had a midlands railway stamp on it. The address was under the name of 'Mrs Thomas, of Piggott's road number 26, Caversham'. The search had now officially begun.[14]

---

[11] https://www.getreading.co.uk/news/berkshire-history/victorian-crime-reading-ameliadyer-

[12] Berkshire Chronicle, 18 April 1896. Viewed 27/02/2017.

[13] http://historybytheyard.co.uk/baby_farming.htm

[14] Angela Buckley, *Amelia Dyer and the Baby Farm Murders*. (Reading, Manor Vale Associates, 2016), p. 4

Reading had been an important market town due to the transport links between towns in the Thames Valley.[15] There were roads, river canals and railway links.[16] After detective Anderson had decoded the washed-out handwriting on the parcel, he took it to the railway station to see if any of the details were familiar to any of the staff. Luckily for the detective, but unluckily for Dyer, the clerk recognised the parcel. However, it was from a different name faintly still on show, it was that of Amelia Dyer, currently residing at 45 Kensington Road.[17] A tightly packed road with a row of terraced houses backing onto the workhouse, this area housed most of the poorest inhabitants.[18] The fact that Dyer was able to carry on her practice over the years pretty much unhindered, was due in no small fact to a failure in the legislation, as the critic Chris Payne explains. According to Payne, "In 1871, the government set up a Select Committee on the Protection of Infant Life, and their recommendations were later included in the Infant Life Protection Act 1872."[19] "However," Payne states, "local authorities were erratic in putting the measures into practice, one terrible consequence of this failure was the case of Amelia Dyer whose serial

---

[15] Buckley, *Amelia Dyer and the Baby Farm Murders*. P. 5.

[16] Buckley, *Amelia Dyer and the Baby Farm Murders*. P. 5.

[17] Buckley, *Amelia Dyer and the baby farm murders*. P. 6.

[18] Buckley, *Amelia Dyer and the baby farm murders*. P. 6.

[19] Chris Payne. *The* Chieftain: *Victorian True Crime through the Eyes of a Scotland Yard Detective. (*Stroud: The History Press, 2011), p. 131.

infanticide shocked the nation in 1896."[20] Jeremy Paxman's book, *The Victorians: Britain Through the Paintings of the Age Accounts for the Victorian Era and its Traces in Today's World and Imagination,* mentions Amelia Dyer's wicked deeds, but he also discusses the difficult conditions Victorian women negotiated in relation to sexuality and childbirth, and the stigma of having a child outside marriage; all factors that contributed to the practice of baby farming.[21] An analysis of the literary language used to elaborate and exaggerate the physical and psychological trademark of Dyer, as illustrative of the female baby farmer. This is key to an examination of the spreading construction of femininity and crime in true crime, and in Rattle and Vale's *The Woman Who Murdered Babies for Money: The Story of Amelia Dyer*. This discussion further investigates these ideologically driven portrayals and the wider problems surrounding the representation of true crime and questions of gender, authenticity and realism.

Dyer's appearance and looks are described in such a way as to emphasise her symbolic, demonised function: described by Rattle and Vale, "The middle-aged, slightly coarse-looking woman who answered the door suspiciously, her heavily built figure filling the doorway. Her dirty brown hair, streaked with grey, was dragged back severely from a centre parting into an untidy bun. She had a deeply lined, almost masculine face, a fleshy chin and loosely drooping eyelids. The straight, hard

---

[20] Chris Payne. *The* Chieftain*: Victorian True Crime through the Eyes of a Scotland Yard Detective. (*Stroud: The History Press, 2011), p. 131.

[21] Jeremy Paxman. The Victorians: Britain through the Paintings of the Age. *(BBC Books; Reprint edition: 2010),* p. 148.

set of her mouth and a glimpse of blackened tooth stumps did nothing to warm her features."[22]

In Rattle and Vale's true crime narrative, Amelia Dyer's mental health as well as her physical representation is characterised in negative terms, as a means of establishing her evil nature, and as an explanatory factor for her serial killings. In both books written about Dyer by Vale, Rattle and Buckley, all suggest uncertainty regarding Dyer's mental health, unsure of whether she was genuinely mentally ill, or it was just a ruse to take light away from her actions. During an episode of mental illness in 1891, Dyer is described in the following terms by Rattle and Vale:

"She was unkempt, her skin filthy, her hair feral, her teeth decaying, blackened or entirely missing. Her tongue dirty and thickly coated. She ranted incessantly, spitting in fury, fuelled by terror, and repeating over and over that the voices in her head wouldn't rest until she has brought about her own annihilation."[23]

The Woman Who Murdered Babies for Money: The Story of Amelia Dyer features the 'maternal' persona of Amelia Dyer in several ways – describing Dyer's relationship with her own daughter Polly, and frequent use of the term 'Mother' to refer to Dyer. Rattle and Vale write, "Whether 'Mother's' suicidal and delusional paranoia was feigned or laudanum-induced is now impossible to tell, but for two weeks her

---

[22] Alison Rattle and Allison Vale, *the woman who murdered Babies for money, the story of Amelia Dyer.* (London, Carlton publishing group 2011), pp. 18-19.

[23] Vale, *the woman who murdered Babies for money, the story of Amelia Dyer,* pp. 99-100.

terrifying frenzy continued."[24] Polly became the focus of Mother's fury and became accustomed to Mother's threats against her, but things became worse and more sinister when 'Mother' threw a knife at her head.[25] The symbol of the 'ideal mother' was dominant in Victorian society and culture. As the critics Claudia C. Klaver and Ellen Bayuk Rosenman state, in their introduction to the book *Other Mothers: Beyond the Maternal Ideal:*

"The virtues of the middle-class woman and of the home over which she was to preside emanated from an image of the mother as pure, self-sacrificing, and devoted, a spiritual influence and a moral instructress."[26] Amelia Dyer is presented as a 'demonic mother', a baby farmer and a serial killer. In the book, *British Serial Killers*, by Nigel Wier, he investigates several infamous criminals, including Amelia Dyer. What is interesting about his book is the way he uses conclusive terminology associated with the breakdown terms of serial killers, the larger number are men according to his investigation. To discuss intensely the female and private sphere, Wier explains that: "A serial killer is typically defined 'as an individual who has murdered three or more people over a period of more than thirty days'."[27] Even though Amelia Dyer's case is clear and terrifying, baby farming cannot be

---

[24] Vale, *The Woman Who Murdered Babies for Money, The Story of Amelia Dyer*, p. 99.

[25] Vale, *The Woman Who Murdered Babies for Money*, p. 99.

[26] Claudia C. Klaver, Rosenma and Ellen Bayuk, *Other Mothers: Beyond the Maternal Ideal.*

(Columbus: Ohio State University Press, 2008), p.2.

[27] Nigel Wier, *British Serial Killers.* (Bloomington, IN: Author House, 2011), p. 11.

reduced to one evil human, but instead needs to be recognised as a social and cultural practice.

As Polly described that 'Mother' was disturbed by the police calling at their house, Dyer attempted suicide by cutting her throat with the same knife she used to peel potatoes. Dyer continuously used to say that the voices told her to do it along with the paranoia affects from laudanum abuse.[28] Eventually Dyer's husband, William, called for a doctor to asses her mental state, the GP's notes say, as stated by Rattle and Vale, "Dyer is on the verge of a mental collapse, she is stout-fat and a flabby woman with her skin thick and coarse, black and decaying teeth with filthy skin."[29] Dyer was subsequently referred to the county asylum in Gloucester. Not surprisingly, Dyer's character had changed since her meeting with the general practitioner in the morning, going from abusive and hallucinating to 'dull, quiet and orderly' with the voices having conveniently stopped.[30] Rattle and Vale state, "Was she recovering from a laudanum binge, or was she playing a shrewd game?"[31] Aware of her surroundings, she was able to enjoy the best an asylum had to offer. Eventually, she was discharged and returned home by train. The lengthy description of Dyer's physical appearance and body language

---

[28] Alison Rattle and Allison Vale, *the woman who murdered Babies for money, the story of Amelia Dyer.* (London, Carlton publishing group 2011), pp. 98-99.

[29] Vale, *the woman who murdered Babies for money, the story of Amelia Dyer.* P. 98.

[30] Vale, *the woman who murdered Babies for money, the story of Amelia Dyer.* P. 101.

[31] Vale, *the woman who murdered Babies for money*, p. 102.

draws on literary echoes for impact.[32] Dyer's portrayal reflects the conventional image of the fairy tale witch, who is described in the following way by Donald Haas, "In popular imagination, which has been influenced by fairy-tale illustrations and animation, the witch has an ugly physical appearance, aligning her in the iconography of the classical fairy-tale with the realm of evil."[33]

"WANTED – Highly respectable married couple wish to ADOPT child: good home. Premium required £10. c/o Bates, Handy & Co: Valpy St Reading."[34]

Western Daily Press, 20 August 1985

Author Dorothy Haller writes in her book, "This ad may have been misleading to the public, but it read like a coded message to unwed mothers. The information about the character and financial condition of the person soliciting for nurse children appears to be acceptable at first glance, but no name is given. No references are asked for and none are offered. The lump sum of £10 to keep an infant or a sickly child was inadequate, and a sickly child and an infant under two months were the least likely to survive and the cheapest to bury. Infants were taken, no questions asked and it was understood that for 10 pounds no questions were expected to

---

[32] Charlotte Beyer, *True Crime and Baby Farming: Representing Amelia Dyer. (2015), pp. 101117.*

[33] Donald Haase, *The Greenwood Encyclopedia of Folktales and Fairy Tales. (Westport, CT:*
Greenwood Press, 2008), p. 1038.

[34] Vale, *the woman who murdered Babies for money*, p. 144.

be asked. The transaction between the mother and the baby farmer usually took place in a public place, on public transportation, or through a second party. No personal information was exchanged, the money was paid, and the transaction was complete. The mother knew deep down she would never see her infant again. Ten pounds was a great deal of money for a young girl on her own, but baby farmers were interested in only one thing: how much money have you got?"[35]

Inhuman crimes, the figures of baby farmers caused more outrage from the public than those women who brawled in the streets or committed murders.

Baby farmers were a contradiction of what Victorian society expected of a woman, the Victorian woman should be a caring mother unlike the baby farmer who neglected and destroyed what the idealistic woman is sworn to protect.[36] In Victorian England, single mothers were judged harshly, unable to find employment, they were surrounded by shame and poverty.[37] Often, they were left no other option than to leave their children in the care of a baby-farmer. Dyer took full advantage of women in these situations, as the practice

---

[35] Dorothy L. Haller, *Bastardy and Baby Farming in Victorian England.* This paper was selected by the Department of History as the Outstanding Paper for the 1989-1990 academic year. P.4.

[36] Lucy Williams, *Wayward Woman – Female Offending in Victorian England.* (Barnsley, Pen & sword 2016), p. 90.

[37] Alison Rattle and Allison Vale, *The Woman who Murdered Babies for Money, The Story of Amelia Dyer.* (London, Carlton publishing group 2011), p. 13.

was unregulated, it was an easy way for Dyer to make a quick wage.[38] Written in *The Independent* on UK crime,

"The world which enabled this wholesale trade in infant life may seem entirely alien today, but its scars are remarkably recent. Our Dickensian vision of Victorian urban filth is missing one grim detail: the bodies of dead infants littered the streets of British cities and reports of their discovery were too commonplace to be considered newsworthy."[39]

The Crime Museum Online explains that, "At the time the Poor Law Amendment Act of 1834 made it, so fathers of illegitimate children were not obligated by law to support their children financially, leaving many women without options."[40] Dyer had learned that from her earlier conviction, that when she returned to baby farming she did not involve any physicians. So, she began disposing of the bodies herself to avoid any added risk. Additionally, she relocated frequently to avoid suspicion and took up the use of aliases.

Horrors in Reading – many victims had been found near Clappers pool; the body pulled from the river was at an advanced state of decomposition.

"The body of another has been recovered today from the Thames, making it the seventh. About noon today, Police

---

[38] Vale, *The Woman who Murdered Babies for Money, The Story of Amelia Dyer.* (London, Carlton publishing group 2011), p. 9.

[39] https://www.independent.co.uk/news/uk/crime/amelia-dyer-the-woman-who-murdered300-babies-8507570.html.

[40] https://www.crimemuseum.org/crime-library/serial-killers/amelia-dyer/. [41] Angela Buckley, *Amelia Dyer and the Baby Farm Murders.* (Reading, Manor Vale Associates, 2016), p. 64.

constable saw a suspicious looking parcel entangled in weeds and on securing it, he found that it contained a body, of a well-developed male child, about twelve months old. The neck, as in the same as the other infants found was tightly tied linen material. The body had appeared in brown paper as several of the other bodies had been."[41]

Evening Post,
1896.

Although the police had matched the double tape around the infants neck to the previous bodies found, the coroner had decided, unfortunately, there was not enough evidence to determine the cause of death to be strangulation, so ruled verdict 'found drowned'.[42] Although it had been fifty years since the first appointed Scotland Yard detectives, relatively few resources were available in 1896 to assist them on any murder investigations.[43] Forensic and crime scenes were still in their infancy, and DNA testing would not available for another century.[44] In the nineteenth century, the most famous fictional character detective Sherlock Holmes, had to rely on characteristics that were physical to identify victims. These included dental records, and distinguishing marks, but as all of Amelia Dyer's victims were infants, this proved difficult to

---

[41] https://www.britishnewspaperarchive.co.uk/
viewer/bl/0001384/18960501/075/0004

[42] Angela Buckley, *Amelia Dyer and the Baby Farm Murders.* (Reading, Manor Vale Associates, 2016), p. 72.

[43] Buckley, *Amelia Dyer and the Baby Farm Murders.* P.71.

[44] Buckley, *Amelia Dyer and the Baby Farm Murders.* P.71.

do.[45] Dyer was arrested following the numerous discoveries of infants and her address still visible upon the brown paper bag along with her alias, Mrs Harding. Dyer was finally remanded at Reading Gaol. The prison was built in 1844, along the banks of the river, this was one of many 'new design prison'.[46] Amelia Dyer was to spend the next four weeks of her life here. She was in one of the thirty cells that housed female drunks and prostitutes. In Rattle and Vale's book, they write in detail of prison conditions, "The cells were dismal, dimly lit and measured only thirteen-feet by seven-feet with a tiny slit as a window. A dented washbasin and small WC lurking in the corner of the room. The harsh regime was soul destroying."[47] Dyer spent her time in Reading prison in relative comfort, surrounded by her personal belongings and provided with decent food along with her books, often reading her favourite book *East Lynne,* a classic Victorian melodrama.[48] The astonishing amount of activity on the river attracted the observations of many inquisitive passers-by. By now rumours and gossip had spread, and the people of Reading heard that a woman was being held at the Gaol, a woman who had used the river in which to dump young infants' bodies.

---

[45] Buckley*, Amelia Dyer*. P.71.

[46] Alison Rattle and Allison Vale*, The Woman who Murdered Babies for Money, The Story of Amelia Dyer.* (London, Carlton publishing group 2011), p. 190.

[47] *Rattle and Vale, The Woman who Murdered Babies for Money, The Story of Amelia Dyer. P.*

[48] Rattle and Vale*, the story of Amelia Dyer*. P. 192. [50] Rattle and Vale*, the story of Amelia Dyer*. P. 197.

"Up to Saturday five bodies have been taken from the Thames. All having met their deaths in a similar manner by strangulation with a piece of tape, then the bodies placed in a parcel with a brick then deposited in the Thames. It is said that thirty or forty infants were found drowned in the Thames within the London district in the last year."[49]

Berkshire Chronicle,
Saturday 18 April 1896.

The walls for Dyer were starting to close in, with increasing evidence building up against her, all she could do was sit in the dock and listen. Letters were found at Dyer's address on Kensington Road that had led the police to contact Evelina Marmon, a barmaid from Cheltenham.

EVALINA EDITH MARMAON. "I live in Cheltenham – in January, this year, I was confined of a female child – in March I saw an advertisement in a Bristol paper, of which this (produced) is a copy: 'Couple with no child, want care of or would adopt one: terms £10. Care of Ship Exchange, Bristol' – 'I wrote 20th: Kensington Road, Oxford Road, Reading, Berks. To Mrs. Scott'.[50] (See plate 1)

'In reference to your letter of adoption of a child, I beg to say I shall be glad to have a little baby girl, one that I can

[49] Rattle and Vale, *the story of Amelia Dyer*. P. 198.

[50] *Old Bailey proceedings online, (*
https://www.oldbaileyonline.org/browse.jsp?id=t18960518-451&div=t18960518-&terms=amelia_dyer#highlight) 18th May 1896, trial of Amelia Elizabeth Dyer, (REF: t18960518-451).

bring up and call my own. First, I must tell you, we are plain, homely people, in good circumstances. We live in our own house and have a good and comfortable home. We are out in the country, and sometimes I am alone a great deal. I don't want the child for money's sake, but for company and home comfort. I and my husband are dearly fond of children. None of my own. A child with me would have a good home, and a mother's love and care. We belong to the Church of England. I would not mind the mother or any friend coming to see the child at any time, and know the child is going on all right. I only hope we may come to terms. I should like to have the baby as soon as you can arrange it. If I can come for her, I don't mind paying for one way. I could break my journey at Gloucester; I have a friend in the Asylum there I should be so glad to call and see. If you will let me have an early reply I can give you some references. – Yours, MARY HARDING.' – I replied to that letter, and received this, dated March 22nd."[51]

Evelina Marmon was the first witness to take the stand, stating she had given birth to a girl she named Doris in January, 1896. There are reports that Marmon was greatly distressed throughout her testimony. She explained she had seen advertisements in the *Bristol Times* and *Mirror* from a couple seeking to adopt a child.[52] By this point Amelia Dyer

[51] *Old Bailey proceedings online, (*
https://www.oldbaileyonline.org/browse.jsp?id=t18960518-451&div=t18960518-&terms=amelia_dyer#highlight) 18th May 1896, trial of Amelia Elizabeth Dyer, (REF: t18960518-451).
[52] Angela Buckley, *Amelia Dyer and the baby farm murders.* (Reading, Manor Vale Associates, 2016), p. 60.

had a solicitor, (see plate 2) it was only by the end of the nineteenth century the state provided defence lawyers, but only for those charged with murder.[53] Many witnesses came forward in the witness stand, mothers who had released their children to this evil monster under the false pretence they would be well cared for, the repeat of the same adverts and correspondence back and forth. As can be seen, the letters are convincing (see plate 3). For a mother in turmoil to receive such reassuring correspondence, it is very clear to see why these mothers let their children go to 'a kind, nurturing mother, Dyer had claimed to be'.

"Publicity given to the case has caused many anxious enquiries to be made to the reading police by persons who have entrusted children to Mrs Dyer's care. Four women who had given her children and premiums have been to the borough to claim the children. They could not, however, be found, but pieces of clothing found in box in Dyer's house have been recognised as parts of the outfits of these children."[54]

Reading Observer, Friday 17 April 1896.

In detail Rattle and Vale state, "Amelia Dyer stared at the floor as she was charged with the murders of Helena Fry, Doris Marmon and Harry Simmons. The circumstances of the case were so grave, it was proposed that the prisoners should

---

[53] Angela Buckley, *Amelia Dyer and the baby farm murders*. p. 67.
[54] Alison Rattle and Allison Vale, *The Woman Who Murdered Babies for Money, The Story of Amelia Dyer*. (London, Carlton publishing group 2011), p. 206.

be remanded in custody for a further week."[55] Dyer's plea of insanity was probably a last-ditch attempt to save herself from the gallows. She admitted her crimes saying, "You will know all mine by the tape around their necks."[56] A doctor who came to examine Dyer was adamant she was a person of a sound mind and responsible for her actions.

She was, however, suffering from opium withdrawal. We must consider she did not fall apart when killing these infants, it was not until the police started to get suspicious of her that she feigned madness in order to save her own neck. This would have been a straightforward capital sentence until Dyer's struggling council decided to enter an insanity plea.[57] Within only five minutes, the jury delivered its verdict: the woman was guilty, and she should hang.[58] Dyer was taken to Newgate Gaol to await her execution.[59]

"I wish the world could understand what it is to have someone saying to you 'get rid of them, get rid of them'. I don't feel mad now, it's so nice and quiet here… I used to like to watch them with the tapes around their neck, but it was soon over with them; though when I had thrown them in the

---

[55] Alison Rattle and Allison Vale, *The Woman Who Murdered Babies for Money, The Story of Amelia Dyer.* p. 207.

[56] Rattle and Vale, *The Woman Who Murdered Babies for Money, The Story of Amelia Dyer.* P. 231.

[57] David, J, Vaughan. *Mad or Bad, Crime and Insanity in Victorian Britain.* (Barnsley, Pen and Sward Ltd, 2017), p. 87.

[58] Vaughan. *Mad or Bad, Crime and Insanity in Victorian Britain.* P.91.

[59] Alison Rattle and Allison Vale, *The Woman Who Murdered Babies for Money, The Story of Amelia Dyer.* (London, Carlton publishing group 2011), p. 238.

water I felt better and easier in mind...before I die I want you to tell the mothers of the little babies that I pray for them every night to forgive me in their hearts."[60] – Extract from an interview with Amelia Dyer by a journalist from the *Weekly Dispatch* from Newgate Gaol.

The insanity defence – this was not unusual but not often successful, the insanity defence is a topic that has brought about much outrage and disapproval from the public. This public outcry would appear to be the product of highly publicised insanity cases and the public not understanding what happens when someone is found, 'not guilty by reason of insanity'.[61] Today, a small playground, has been built in an ivy-shadowed area next to a stonewall. None of the residents know that surrounding the echoes of laughter from the children playing, underneath their feet of tanbark lie fragments of long forgotten remains of countless murderers and madmen from Newgate Prison.[62] "To understand the scale of capital punishment at Newgate Prison, it is said that between 1790 and 1902 over one thousand people were put to death there. During the period of public executions, these

---

[60] Rattle and Vale, *The Woman Who Murdered Babies for Money, The Story of Amelia Dyer.*

(London, Carlton publishing group 2011), p. 238.

[61] Kristen R. Neville, *The Insanity Defense: A Comparative Analysis.* (Eastern Michigan University, 2010). Senior Honours' Theses. 244. http://commons.emich.edu/honors/244.

[62] Kelly Grovier, *The Goal; the story of Newgate prison, London's most notorious Prison.* (London, A Hachette UK Company, 2009), pp. xiii-xiv.

were carried out outside of Newgate Prison on the Old Bailey Road."[63] Published in the Historic History Magazine,

"The church of St Sepulchre-without-Newgate also has a rather ghoulish part to play in the executions. At midnight on the eve of an execution, a bellman would walk along the prison the church of St Sepulchre-without-Newgate also has a rather ghoulish part to play in the executions. At midnight on the eve of an execution, a bellman would walk along the prison."[64]

This would have been what Dyer heard at the eve of her own execution, in the walls of this dismal and gloomy prison. Every detail of the execution carried out was recorded regarding Dyer, from the rope around her neck, to the name of her executioner, James Billingham, (See plate 4). Therein followed a certificate from the surgeon examining the death of Amelia Dyer (See plate 5). Executions had not been carried out in public since 1868, so Dyer would meet her end within the prison walls. Four to five hundred people gathered, and a black flag was raised to signal the death of Dyer, with many cheers.[65] Amelia Dyer's body hung for an hour, until she was cut down and placed in front of a jury ready for viewing from the inquest. Her execution had been carried out to satisfaction

---

[63] https://www.historic-uk.com/HistoryMagazine/DestinationsUK/Newgate-Prison-Wall/.
[64] https://www.historic-uk.com/HistoryMagazine/DestinationsUK/Newgate-Prison-Wall/.
[65] Angela Buckley, *Amelia Dyer and the baby farm murders*. (Reading, Manor Vale Associates, 2016), p. 93.

with the Newgate's medical officer concluding her death was due to a dislocated neck.[66] (See plate 6-7).

Legal repercussions – the horrific crimes of Dyer were too great to be ignored by the Home Office.[67] As we have seen, the reader's affect and emotional identification are central aspects in the complex dynamic of these true crime narratives. They play on and exploit the reader's inability to 'look away', as shame, guilt, anger, disbelief, and abjection are provoked by their images and narratives. Yet it is important to remember that these true crime stories also examine and re-present documented historical realities.[68] True crime exposes the hypocrisy of Victorian society and exploits the contemporary reader's responses of powerlessness and disbelief. In *The Woman Who Murdered Babies for Money: The Story of Amelia Dyer,* the insistence on historical distance helps to alienate and detach the reader from what they are observing, by allowing them to hide behind an attitude of enlightenment. But at the same time, the question persists.[69] Due to the outrage caused by Amelia Dyer's case and the magnitude of her baby killings, the authorities were finally forced to intervene. The Home Office introduced new, tighter legislation for the care and welfare of children, and imposed

---

[66] Angela Buckley, *Amelia Dyer and the Baby Farm Murders*. P. 93.

[67] Alison Rattle and Allison Vale, *The Woman Who Murdered Babies for Money, The Story of Amelia Dyer.* (London, Carlton publishing group 2011), p. 245.

[68] Charlotte Beyer, *True Crime and Baby Farming: Representing Amelia Dyer. (2015), pp. 101117.*

[69] *Ruth Paley and, Simon Fowler.* Family Skeletons: Exploring the Lives of our Disreputable Ancestors. *(Kew: National Archives, 2005), p. 26.*

a responsibility for local authorities to regulate and inspect houses and individuals suspected of involvement in baby farming.[70] Rattle and Vale establish the importance and impact of the work done by NSPCC to rescue children from this kind of fate. The book contrasts the terrible images of child cruelty and described by Rattle and Vale, "Photographs of the same children, the rescued ones, taken months later: plump-cheeked and smiling, dressed in clean, stiff jackets and sitting straight-backed on the photographer's chair. Those found alive, in whatever deplorable condition, were the lucky ones."[71] These painful and distorted images of the effect of child cruelty are extremely disturbing, not merely because of their factual and historical accuracy, but because of the emotional acknowledgement they provoke, even demand from the reader. Such images are frequent throughout Rattle and Vale's book, exposing the reader to the harsh realities of baby farming. Across the historical distance of more than a century and immense social and cultural changes, these graphic pictures of child cruelty still profoundly affect the modern reader. Author Angela Buckley states that, "One hundred and twenty years later, Amelia Dyer's story is tightly woven into Reading's history. In 1908, the Children's Act was passed, introducing the legal registration of foster parents and allotting additional powers to local authorities to protect

---

[70] Alison Rattle and Allison Vale, *The Woman Who Murdered Babies for Money, The Story of Amelia Dyer.* (London, Carlton publishing group 2011), p. 246.
[71] Alison Rattle and Allison Vale, *The Woman Who Murdered Babies for Money, The Story of Amelia Dyer.* (London, Carlton publishing group 2011), p. 12.

vulnerable children within their care."[72] The bridge has been long gone and there is no longer any memorial for the babies that perished at the hands of Amelia Dyer.[73]

[72] Angela Buckley, *Amelia Dyer and the Baby Farm Murders*. (Reading, Manor Vale Associates, 2016), p. 97.

[73] Angela Buckley, *Amelia Dyer and The Baby Farm Murders*. P. 98.

Chapter Two
The Brutal Side to the Fairer Sex

In Victorian England, the divide between men and women was very clear. Lucy Williams writes, "It was an era where men were expected to live up to traditional ideals of masculinity and women were expected to achieve the feminine ideal."[74] While we think of Victorian women, with big dresses and impeccable manners, crime and deviance are often the last thing to spring to mind. Surely characters such as Amelia Dyer are a one off, or few and far between? Zedners describes that, "In Victorian England, women made up a far larger proportion of those known to be involved in crime than they do today; the nature of female criminality attracted considerable attention and preoccupied those trying to provide for women within the penal system."[75] The Victorians found that they had their fair share of 'wayward women', my

---

[74] Lucy Williams, *Wayward Woman – Female Offending in Victorian England.* (Barnsley, Pen & sword 2016), p. ix.

[75] Lucia Zedner, *Woman, Crime and Custody in Victorian England.* (Oxford, Clarendon Press, 1991), Introduction summary.

aim in this chapter is to provide narratives of death and deception of inhuman murderesses.[76]

Gender, as a category of analysis, has become deeply embedded within women's history offering an imaginary tool which is used to delve and explore the arrangement of sexual difference that are ingrained in all societies. Indeed, the idea of gender has challenged the very notion of a 'women's history' that is conceived as a narrow project, for it questions the extent to which women can be studied in isolation from the experiences of men and discourages the treatment of women as a unified group pursuing common aims, interests and occupations.[77] Zedner's crime book says, "Prostitution and alcoholism were particularly condemned as 'moral crimes', and portrayed as women's 'true' nature and social obligations."[78] Kermode and Walker suggest that the gendered categorisation of crime needs to be more fully improved. An exclusive focus on 'female' crimes, however,

---

[76] Lucy Williams, *Wayward Woman – Female Offending in Victorian England.* (Barnsley, Pen & sword 2016), introduction page.

[77] *These ideas have been particularly elaborated by Joan Scott and Denise Riley who have advocated the study of the social meanings of gender through an analysis of language and discourse:*
J. Wallach Scott, *Gender and the Politics of History*, (Columbia University Press, 1988), Denise Riley, *"Am I That Name?" Feminism and the Category of "women" in History, (Macmillan, 1988).*

[78] Lucia Zedner, *Women, Crime and Custody in Victorian England,* (Clarendon, 1991), p. 2. [82] Jenny Kennode and Gailbine Walker, *Women, Crime and the Courts in Early Modern England*, (UCL Press Ltd., 1994), p. 20.

may reproduce and reinforce this labelling effect if we do not also explore the treatment of those women whose offences were considered to contradict their very nature. Introducing *Women, Crime and the Courts'* editors Kermode and Walker, they not only point to the gendered labelling of criminal activity in criminology but highlight the contrasting categorisation and responses to crimes committed by men and women. Men who commit crimes are more likely to be defined as 'criminal', their motives rational, economic and explicable; women, on the other hand, are frequently represented as mentally ill, irrational or insane.[79] Judith Walkowitz's study of Victorian prostitution. Her analysis differentiates between the values and interests of a dominant culture within which the prostitute was defined in various pathological and moral terms as a 'miserable creature' or a 'depraved temptress'.[80] The meaning which prostitutes and their own class, attached to their 'sexual deviancy' by focusing on economic conditions and the urban environment, Walkowitz can show that prostitutes tended to be 'unskilled daughters of the unskilled classes', and that their entry into

---

[79] *Radojka Startup, Damaging Females: Representations of Women as Victims and Perpetrators of Crime in the Mid-Nineteenth Century.* (Submitted for the degree of Doctor of Philosophy to the Department of History, University College London, February 2000), p.22.

[80] *Radojka Startup, Damaging Females: Representations of Women as Victims and Perpetrators of Crime in the Mid-Nineteenth Century. Pp, 24-25.*

the trade often represented a rational choice in the face of severely limited options and general exploitation.[81]

To start with, I would like to talk about a slightly different type of female criminal, 'the garrotting gang'. These were not murderesses but still very much a degrading crime to a man, these were dark and dangerous times in urban areas. Storey writes, "In the nineteenth century, London was gripped by a garrotting scare."[82] These woman often posed as prostitutes so they had a better chance of getting closer to their victims and then luring them down a dark alley; the victim would be punched in the throat and an accomplice would come out from behind him, strangling him to the point of passing out before stealing from him, items such as a wallet and or a watch.[83] In particular, the so-called 'garrotting' cases, where often using their arm or a length of wire, cord, or cloth, seemed to touch a raw nerve with the people of London, with the fear of garrotting reaching a fever-pitch in the 1860s. Parliament pushed through the 'Security from Violence Act' in 1863. Under the terms of this new act of Parliament, criminals convicted of any violent theft could be punished with 'up to 50 lashes' along with a hefty prison sentence.[84] The weird thing about garrotting and how widely it was reported at the time, is that it doesn't actually appear to have been all that

---

[81] Judith Walkowitz, *Prostitution and Victorian Society: Women, Class and the State,* (Cambridge, Cambridge University Press, 1980), p. 15.

[82] Neil. R Storey, *The Victorian Criminal.* (Oxford, Shire Publications Ltd, 2011), p. 22.

[83] R Storey, *The Victorian Criminal.* P. 22.

[84]*http://www.todayifoundout.com/index.php/2015/06/garrotting-panic-1850-insane-wayspublic-reacted/.*

common; even during the supposed height of the 'garrotting panic of 1862'. So why the panic? As it turns out, although garrotting itself was never a major problem in London, newspapers from the era positively *loved* reporting on it. This led to the few isolated cases that did happen being blown way out of proportion and reported on to such an extent that the people of London were led to believe the streets were filled to the brim with roving rabbles of ruffians armed with lengths of wire.[85]

Women accused of wrongdoing held a special fascination for the Victorians. Their blend of passion, eroticism, and danger served to spark the Victorian imagination. The ideal Victorian woman, or the 'angel of the house' was defined by her role within the home because the family served as a sanctuary for the "preservation of traditional moral and religious values," states Zedner.[86] The qualities valued by Victorian society in the ideal female were submissiveness, innocence, purity, gentleness, self-sacrifice, patience, modesty, passivity and altruism. "The middle-class Victorian woman was to have no ambition other than to please others and care for her family,"[87] as described clearly by Zedner. According to the Victorian ideal, a woman was to be "a

---

[85] *http://www.todayifoundout.com/index.php/2015/06/garrotting-panic-1850-insane-wayspublic-reacted/.*

[86] Lucia Zedner. *Women, Crime and Custody in Victorian England.* (Oxford: Oxford University press, 1991), p. 12.

[87] Zedner. *Women, Crime and Custody in Victorian England.* P. 15.

monument of selflessness, with no existence beyond the loving influence she exuded as daughter, wife, and mother."[88]

Maunder and Moore write, "The face of crime in nineteenth century Britain was changing. The establishment of a police force in 1829 and a detective force in 1842 indicates that the detection and apprehension of criminals was becoming a greater priority."[89] Female violence is excused not only with heredity, but also with the rise of industrialism, poverty, and limited job opportunities for women.

In *Child Sexual Abuse in Victorian England*, Louise Jackson writes, "morality, industry and virtue were closely related; economic failure was both a result and a sign of idleness and moral deficiency."[90] This resonates with the Amelia Dyer case; poverty and no job opportunities forces vulnerable women to turn to baby farmers, unaware of exactly who they were selling their child too.

"One of the most renowned achievements of the Victorian age is the birth of the modern prison system, the rise of these prisons became a dominant part of punishment. Gaols and lock ups did exist but always acted as no more than holding pens for those awaiting trial."[91]

---

[88] Nina Auerbach, *Woman and the Demon: The Life of a Victorian Myth. (*Boston: Harvard University Press, 1982), p. 185.

[89] Andrew Maunder and Grace Moore. *"Introduction." Victorian Crime, Madness and*

Sensation. (Hampshire and Burlington: Ashgate, 2004), p. 1

[90] Louise Jackson*, Child Sexual Abuse in Victorian England. (*London: Routledge, 2000), 107.

[91] Lucy Williams*, Wayward Woman. (*Barnsley, Pen & Sward books Ltd, 2016), p. 2. [96] P. King*, 'Female Offenders, Work and Life-Cycle*

The role of gender in the optional process in the late eighteenth and early nineteenth centuries went unremarked until recently. As late as 1996, it was possible to say that historians of crime in England in the eighteenth and early nineteenth centuries had given little attention to the role of gender and had "found it remarkably difficult to give their work a properly contextualised gender dimension," states King. The history of criminology combined the relative neglect of female offenders, being unable to engage with issues of gender until late in the twentieth century. Studies concentrated on women's social and moral situation, and their vulnerability to 'falling' into crime and defiance. History was a man's truth; women were outside of this territory and from the outset were 'unequal'. Before 1930, women were generally documented in mainstream history through a 'sex-stereotypical lens'.[92] Female criminals have always been constructed as 'doubly deviant'; seen to have breached two sets of laws, the laws of the land which forbids violence and the 'natural' laws, which holds that women must be passive carers, mothers and wives; moral beings not active aggressors, a role of which is delegated to men.[93] Therefore, to have a female criminal is to immediately label an 'other', a woman outside of the 'natural' feminine. "A woman is going

<hr>

in Late Eighteenth-century London', Continuity and Change, 11, (1996), p.61.

[92] J. Purvis, Women's History: Britain, 1850-1945: An Introduction. (New York, UCL press, 1995), p. 5.

[93] A. Lloyd, Doubly Deviant Doubly Damned, Society's Treatment of Violent Women.
(Michigan, Penguin Books, 1995), p. 36.

to be judged not only in the light of the crime she is accused of, but also what kind of woman (mother, sister, wife, daughter) she is deemed to be or whether she is 'mad or bad'," states Lloyd.[94] The killing by a murderess is not presented as an act of what she has done, but as a 'punishment that takes place'.[95] The very activity of the murderess is what she has actually done is replaced with 'what happens'.[96] The woman who kills is presented as being divorced from any agency at all, she may have her behaviour and inner experience documented, but this never amounts to justification or the admittance of a full range of human emotions and reactions. Relating women who kill to mythic characters has the consequence of increasing fear and eliciting harsh responses from society and the legal system. Using 'evil witch' to describe a woman who kills, serves to distance her from her society and her agency becomes that of a character from a storybook, rather than just a woman. This is true when describing Amelia Dyer's appearance, this fits well with her characteristics, she is not petite, attractive or well-mannered but had an evil appearance as well as an evil nature.

In this part of my dissertation I am going to write about another lady, Mary Ann Cotton. I don't plan on writing too much detail about her, but intend to use her as an example, of another 'evil woman'. It was July 1872 in West Auckland; Mary Ann Cotton attracted the beginning of what was to be

---

[94] A. Lloyd, *Doubly Deviant Doubly Damned, Society's Treatment of Violent Women*. P. 18.

[95] H. Allen, *Justice Unbalanced*. (Open university press, 1987). P. 41.

[96] Allen, *Justice Unbalanced*. P.41.

colossal media attention, in just the same way as Dyer. Mary Ann was born in 1832 in a small mining town of Low Moorsley.[97] The case begins with speculation over the deaths of several family members of 'gastric fever', spanning most of Mary Ann's adult life. A comment made by Mary Ann to the overseer of the village, a Mr Thomas Riley, regarding her stepson being placed into the workhouse, was the catalyst which sparked the suspicion.

Upon Riley's resistance to admit the boy to the workhouse without his mother, she is said to have stated, "it won't matter, I won't be troubled long,"[98] within the week the boy was dead. This coincidence led Riley to inform the police and so the 'West Auckland Poisoning Cases' to proceed. "Women who choose poison as their weapon have, throughout history, been regarded as particularly despicable because their crimes could never be constructed as being due to a sudden and temporary loss of 'self-control'," states Ballinger.[99] This mirrors Dyer's way of murder, a prolonged death, pre-planned and calculated, and all were adults and children in both their care. "Just like Dyer," says Geoffrey Abbotts, "she was no ordinary spur-of-the-moment killer; her murderous instincts had resulted in the deaths of fifteen-twenty people, including children, some of which were her own."[100]

---

[97] S. Webb & M. Brown. *Mary Ann Cotton: Victorian Serial Killer*, (Durham, The Langley Press 2016), p. 10.

[98] *The Watford Observer,* (seen 25/04/2018).

[99] A. Ballinger, *Dead Women Walking: Executed Women in England And Wales, 1900-1955*.
(Ashgate, Dartmouth 2000), p. 165.

[100] Geoffroy Abbott, *Female Executions; Martyrs, Murderesses and Mad Women*. (Chichester, Summerdale Publishers Ltd, 2013), p. 74.

"The child she rocked on her knee today, was poisoned tomorrow."[101] The contrast between Cotton and Dyer is the appearance, we all know the harsh stern unruly look of Dyer, whereas Cotton always appeared to look after her appearance. Dyer killed for money, as did Cotton, who preferred the finer things in life. Abbotts states, "Murderous, though eternally feminine, Mary Ann was determined to look her best even for William Calcroft (her executioner). When the wardress went to escort her from her condemned cell to the scaffold, they found her brushing her long, black hair in front of the mirror. As they approached her, she turned and said brightly: 'Right, now I'm ready!'"[102]

Mary Ann was also a woman without mercy, and quite prepared to administer arsenic to anyone: man, woman or child (including her own) and to watch them die in agony.

In a similar vein to Dyer, her victims were dispensable, trading in one for another as a source of income from insurance claims.[103] As described in the *Auckland Times*, "The wretched woman had hardly been on the platform half a minute before she was launched into eternity."[104] Death, apparently being instantaneous, unlike her victims.

I have argued that what is known about female criminals, not only as criminals but as women, plays a deep-rooted role

[101] Geoffroy Abbott, *Female Executions; Martyrs, Murderesses and Mad Women*. P.74.

[102] Geoffroy Abbott, *Female Executions; Martyrs, Murderesses and Mad Women*. Pp. 74-75.

[103] Neil R. A. Bell, Trevor N Bond, Kate Clarke and M W. Oldridge. *The A-Z of Victorian Crime.*
(Stroud, Amberley Publishing, 2016), p. 93.

[104] *Auckland Times and Herald* 27th March 1873.

in determining how their crimes are constructed. In Victorian hetero-patriarchal society, it is essential to come up with an explanation for criminal women, these women being a danger to the very foundations of Victorian society. When criminal women commit violent crimes, they are seen to have violated two sets of laws, those of nature which insist on the passivity of women and those of the law which forbids violence. This 'doubly deviant' and gender stereotypical label ensures that these women will be punished, whether it is an attack upon their femininity or punishment employed by the state; in most cases it is both.[105] Not only did the women researched, kill when they were supposed to care, but due to the fact that they represent a tiny fraction of serious criminals, their novelty value would always guarantee media interest.[106] Women who seriously offend are the most depraved examples of humanity, judged by the public after reading a media report, who are largely unaware of their actual deviations, these women become symbolically detached from their crimes. Women and criminals as two separate entities, not (as men are) merely criminals. I have demonstrated that the women were not only judged for their crimes, but also for their gendered performance as women. As wife, mother, grandmother, servant or employee, it was upon their reputation that a trial and the media focussed.[107] Women who kill are not victims of

---

[105] A. Lloyd, *Doubly Deviant Doubly Damned, Society's Treatment of Violent Women.* (1995), p.36.

[106] Yvonne Jewkes, *Media and Crime.* (Sage Publications, 2010), p. 121

[107] Judith Butler, *Gender Trouble*. (New York, Routledge, Chapman and Hall Inc., 1990), p. 25.

a biological function, 'evil eccentricity' of womanhood, who can be set apart from the rest of the female sex, of whom are deemed 'normal' (a portrayal which denies rationality and agency behind their crimes). Instead, the behaviour of criminal women is deeply rooted within society, their crimes reflecting the changing social conditions of women.[108] J. M.

Beattie's study of female criminality in England was ground-breaking. He showed clearly that women participated in the same range of offences as men, even though this was in lower numbers. He saw little evidence of supposedly 'natural' feminine weakness and passivity in relation to their involvement in crime.[109] Widely cited works, such as those by Garthine Walker, and the collection of essays edited by Walker and Jenny Kermode, explored the dynamics of a range of crimes, in the light of gendered experiences. Previous views concerning the methods and motives of female crime were challenged, and women's involvement in criminal activity was shown to have been far more complex than earlier historians suggested.[110] "Women were previously considered as victims of violence, usually domestic abuse,"[111] Kilday

---

[108] A. Ballinger, *Dead Women Walking: Executed Women in England and Wales, 1900-1955.* (Ashgate, Dartmouth 2000), p. 127.

[109] J. M. Beattie, *'The Criminality of Women in Eighteenth-Century England', Journal of Social History, 8* (1975), 80-116.

[110] Garthine Walker, *Crime, Gender and Social Order in Early Modern* England (Cambridge: Cambridge University Press, 2003); Kermode and Walker (eds.), *Women, Crime and the Courts.*

[111] J. A. Sharpe, *'Domestic Homicide in Early Modern England', The Historical Journal,* 24 (1981), pp. 29-48.

states, "publications in the last two decades have shown that women were just as capable as men of committing varying degrees of non-fatal, as well as fatal, violence."[112]

"Poison has long been considered a distinctly feminine method of murder," Kilday states. Reginald Scot claimed in the sixteenth century that women were the first inventors and the greatest practisers of poisoning and more materially addicted.[113]

Francis Dolan remarked that "poison was 'the early modern housewife's method of choice' because it was a 'stealthy, tidy, non-confrontational method...'[which] relies on more cunning than physical strength."[114] For Dyer and Cotton, this was undoubtedly manipulation and premeditated. Arsenic is the poison of choice, it's because it goes undetected; it has no taste or colour and is odourless. Hence, why they both went undetected for such a long period of time. The label of insanity provides an example of the likes of many female criminals such as Dyer tried to plead, but this is also evident in the way that society attempted to explain and make sense of their act. The use of the insanity verdict for murderous women was relatively rare in the courts, with only four suspects, between 1730 and 1830, deemed mentally insane, and therefore, not tried or considered responsible for

---

[112] Anne-Marie Kilday, *Women and Violent Crime in Enlightenment Scotland* (Woodbridge:

Boydell Press, 2007), Ch. 3

[113] Reginald Scot, *'The Discoveries of Witchcraft'*, (London, 1584), as cited in *Walker, Crime, Gender and Social Order*, p.144.

[114] Frances E. Dolan, *Dangerous Familiars; Representations of Domestic Crime in England 1550-1700.* (London, Cornell University Press, 1994), p. 30.

their actions. Despite the difficulties in obtaining proof, and the apparent rarity with which madness was used to obtain an acquittal, insanity was still used in contemporary literature to explain a murderous woman's actions, particularly when the victim was a child. Joel Peter Eigen has shown that melancholia came to be used frequently in association with insanity at the Old Bailey by the late-nineteenth century, with almost all suspects said to be suffering from it and targeting their own children.[115] This did not work for the likes of Amelia Dyer and Mary Ann Cotton, murderer of her own children, both of their 'lunacy' were not during their actions but only when authorities caught up with them. Although insanity could not be used to justify the actions of a murderous woman, it appears to have been used in particularly heinous cases to help explain how she could act so contrastingly to her expected gendered behaviour. Although newspapers were quick to label murderesses insane, rarely did the courts acquit on the grounds of insanity.

Women most often killed familiar parties, there is little evidence of 'same-sex' violence, as they fatally attacked both males and females. When acting with another individual, they most commonly appeared alongside men, but not necessarily their spouse. The methods of murder chosen were rarely non-confrontational or underhand, which is partly explicable through the young age of many of their victims. The defendants would have had superior strength, even without the use of a weapon. Female-perpetrated acts of violence frequently took place in, or near, the home, and often stemmed from familial concerns. Unlike men, women rarely

---

[115] Eigen, 'Not their fathers' sons', p. 94.

killed strangers, but members of their close or extended family, or associates. Frances Dolan suggests, "This was not because women remained solely within the home. Female-perpetrated murder has been portrayed as an inversion of women's nurturing role, and their use of poison as a domestic betrayal."[116] Poisoning, asphyxiation and drowning accounted for nearly half of female murder cases and were particularly difficult to identify as they often left no noticeable outward signs of murder, and such deaths could be mistaken as natural. This is another reason why an infamous killer such as Dyer, went undetected for such a long time, so not at all uncommon as a first thought. Lucy Williams suggests that throughout the Victorian period, violent crimes perpetrated by woman remained the minority of female offenders. Despite the sensational reports of cunning lady poisoners dominating the headlines, these crimes were exceptional and not representative overall of female violence in this period.[117] In the final words of Vaughan, "Did mad people suffer, or the guilty escape?"

Storey suggests, "Our fascination with this dark aspect of Victorian Britain is kept alive by the countless books, films and television programs, and while many of the real cases

---

[116] Frances E. Dolan, *Dangerous Familiars: Representations of Domestic Crime in England, 1550-1700* (London: Cornell University Press, 1994), p. 30.

[117] Lucy Williams, *Wayward Woman.* (Barnsley, Pen & Sward books Ltd, 2016), p. 115. [123] David, J, Vaughan. *Mad or Bad, Crime and insanity in Victorian Britain.* (Barnsley, Pen and Sward Ltd, 2017), p. ix.

remain crimes of their time, many others have a clear sonority today."[118]

---

[118] Neil. R Storey, *The Victorian Criminal.* (Oxford, Shire Publications Ltd, 2011), back cover.

Chapter Three
Year of the Ripper

In 1888, Jack the Ripper made the headlines with a series of horrific murders in Whitechapel, London. The first victim of 1888 was a woman named Elizabeth Gibbs on New Year's Day. She lay dying in freezing temperatures with a decapitated right arm and bruising to her face.[119] Medical staff at Hyde park did all they could to save her but with no success, she would be one of 122 murder victims that year, along with over half being female. The victims of the ripper never came to justice as the murderer was never unidentified, but the newspapers were unfortunately only too happy to promote the legend to make a profit turning it into a melodrama in the process. Murder is the ultimate crime, but many murders were often overlooked or just ignored by the press and public because these types of heinous crimes were not uncommon in nineteenth century Britain. In this chapter, I aim to talk about victims of homicide in this year of Victorian London to give an insight into what it might have been like to live through one of the hardest times in our history.

---

[119] Peter Stubley, *1888 London Murders in the Year of the Ripper.* (Stroud, the History Press, 2012), p. 7.

The British Empire was at the height of its influence, not just in London but the world. Inhabitants of this time included many historical figures such as a young Winston Churchill, Florence Nightingale, Oscar Wilde and Joseph Merrick – the elephant man, to name a few. Most important of all ruling all over these was Queen Victoria, the empress of India, with the year previous celebrating her Golden Jubilee. Although Victoria had celebrated the end of 1887 full of enthusiasm and joy, she entered the year of 1888 very differently with the death of her son-in-law, the economy struggling with depression, protestors continue to riot in the streets and a series of murders began moral panic, the year of the Ripper! Close by to the known Whitechapel was Spitalfields, a part of London that was tainted by darkness and misery. Surviving centuries of poverty and despair known as the worst street in London, crime and disease spread through like wild fire with ramshackle houses crammed by overcrowding, with gardens converted into courtyard areas to accommodate more residents. Most woman living here lived a dishonest life, professions of prostitutes and a lifestyle of alcoholics these 'unfortunates' taunted daily. In the year of 1888, Emma Smith was an alcoholic and a street worker. To resort to this profession to fund her drinking habit was her death. She was attacked by a group of men that followed her, assaulted her, beat her then rammed a blunt object inside her rupturing her internal organs. Through her agony Emma managed to get back to her lodgings to alert the deputy, Mary Russell, who was horrified of this brutal attack took her to hospital where she died the next day. Emma was a common prostitute so too insignificant to be reported as anything big, even though the story did make front page of *Lloyds Weekly News* on the

Sunday.[120] Life in the city, London housed more than 10,000 public houses in 1888, this was often just an extra room used by the community just to escape the cold and day-to-day life. The pubs were only used by 'ruffians', no place for a respectable lady or gentleman, with more 16,500 arrests in this year for drunk and disorderly.[121]

London's East End was the 'heart of darkness'. Before Jack the Ripper the mythology of London areas of Whitechapel, Spitalfields and the docks were real, drawing in every beggar, prostitute and crook within the east end radius. This 'plagued' area became more exaggerated when Jack the Ripper started murdering in the autumn, unchecked immigration and sweated labour. Whitechapel had come to represent outcast London, the starvation wages, overcrowding and inhumane poor relief were just a few marked living conditions there. On the 29th September 1888, Punch magazine published one of the most iconic poems of the time, John Tenniel's *Nemesis of Neglect*. This reads as follows:

"There floats a phantom of the slum's foul air, shaping to eyes which have the gift of seeing, into the spectre of that loathly lair face it – for vain is fleeing!

Red-handed, ruthless, furtive, underact, 'tis murderous crime – the nemesis of neglect!"

What Tenniel's poem suggests is that the Ripper was a manifestation in semi human form of the area itself; a

---

[120] Fiona Rule, *Worst Street in London.* (Surrey, Allan Publishing Ltd, 2008), pp. 106-107.

[121] Report of the commissioner of police of the metropolis for the year 1888, p. 27

'phantom' he says, 'of the slum's foul air', a result of leaving Whitechapel to fester in its own filth and depravity. Indeed, as John Marriott has written, this cartoon, along with several other observations and comments in the popular press, helped to reinforce the idea that Whitechapel and 'by extension, East London – was a site of fear, loathing and moral desolation's and as such it represented a very real threat to the entire fabric of late Victorian society and the Empire. As the Whitechapel murders unfolded, the area was invaded by curious onlookers and ghoulish tourists, as well as newspaper reporters desperate for local colour and copy to fill their columns and steal a march on their rivals. However, the press found that the police became increasingly reluctant to talk to them as criticism of their efforts to catch the killer was coupled with wild suggestions as to the identity of culprit and even wilder recommendations of how he might be captured. One consequence of this was that the press and other social commentators turned their attention to the area itself. They peered into the dark unlit courts, mingled with the crowds, visited the soup kitchens and gawped at the strange foreign faces on Middlesex Street and Brick Lane. What they saw alarmed them and there were calls for something to be done. That great socialist thinker, George Bernard Shaw even suggested that the Whitechapel murders had had an unexpected and beneficial side effect in highlighting the social problems of East London. Writing to the *Star* newspaper Shaw commented that:

"Private enterprise has succeeded where Socialism failed. Whilst we conventional Social Democrats were wasting our time on education, agitation, and organisation,

some independent genius has taken the matter in hand, and by
simply murdering and disembowelling four women, converted
the proprietary press to an inept sort of communism."

However, it would be wrong to suggest that the problems of Whitechapel and its environs were somehow 'discovered' in the autumn of 1888; social reformers, radicals, investigative journalists and upper-class 'slummers' had been mooching around the East End for decades.[122] The murders of Jack the Ripper in the autumn of 1888 were confined to a small area of London's East End, but similarly provoked a nation-wide panic whipped up by press sensationalism. Violence, especially violence with a sexual frisson, sold newspapers. But violent crime in the form of murder and street robbery never figured significantly in the statistics or in the courts.[123] The descriptions of the Jack the Ripper victims were just another stereotype, they were old, in poor health and lived in the worst housing type in Victorian London.[124] While many theories surrounding Jack the Ripper point towards these horrific mutilations were carried out by someone with medical knowledge, but was quickly dismissed by medical experts perhaps to sweep away anyone with that profession

---

[122] Gray, D. (2011*) Contextualising the Ripper murders: Poverty, Crime and Unrest in the East*
End of London, 1888. Invited Keynote presented to: Jack the Ripper Through a Wider Lens: An Interdisciplinary Conference, Bossone Research Enterprise Center, Drexel University, Philadelphia, USA, 28-29 October 2011. Pp. 1-2.

[123] www.bbc.co.uk/history/british/victorians/crime_01.shtml.

[124] Peter Stubley, *1888 London murders in the year of the Ripper.* (Stroud, the History press, 2012), p. 141.

could not be associated with such crimes. While the victims died from 'unlawful operations' – illegal abortions, it questions the anatomical knowledge of the killer.

'Do you think that it could be a case not of Jack the Ripper but Jill the Ripper?' The idea was that a midwife would be the only type of woman capable of killing in such a gory way. Rumours that Mary Kelly – Jacks final victim, was pregnant at the time of her death, fed into the theory, due to a midwife's easy access to other women's homes. No one would look twice at a midwife with blood on her clothing, and moreover she could slip away from her crime scenes unnoticed the way the Ripper was notorious for doing. A particularly interesting one is that a midwife would have known how to use pressure points on the neck to render a woman unconscious, which was apparently something that midwives used to do to women in labour back in Victorian England. Thus, begins the theory of Jill the Ripper – sometimes labelled the mad midwife. As ludicrous as it may sound initially, there are several points which add credibility to the theory. First, the fact that all of London was looking for Jack the Ripper (i.e. a man) would allow a female murderer to walk the streets of Whitechapel with considerably less fear of capture or discovery. Second, a midwife would be perfectly common to be seen at all hours of the night. Third, any presence of blood on her clothing would be immediately discarded because of her work. Finally, based on the evidence pointing to an anatomically educated murderer, a midwife would have the anatomical knowledge some believed the murderer possessed. Amelia Dyer, the theory fits with Dyer's cruel disregard for her infant victims and it's highly likely she was still killing babies in 1888. Also, she was a midwife and would have known her way around the

54

female anatomy – Catherine Eddowes' left kidney and uterus were cut out and taken by the killer. And being a midwife, no one would have batted an eyelid if her clothing was bloodstained. If she was found with any of the bodies, as a nurse she could have claimed she was coming to their aid – the perfect cover. With several aliases, Dyer also knew how to hide in plain sight and evaded police for much of her 30-year killing spree. Not trying to solve a nearly 200-year-old unsolvable famous crime, but the 'Jill the Ripper' theory holds a stronger case than 'Jack'. The end of 1888 draws close, London was drowned by dense fog rolling from the Thames. With temperatures falling below zero making all roads icy death traps. As London went into darkness and chaos everyone bolted doors until the next sunrise. This seemed a fitting end to the Ripper year, with London plummeting into the depths of hell with a series of legendary events.

Metropolitan Police Statistics on Murder and Manslaughter 1881-1891:

Year	Population	Murder	Manslaughter
1881	4,788,657	11	84
1882	4,990,952	10	85
1883	5, 042,556	16	83
1884	5,147,727	16	74
1885	5,225,069	9	97
1886	5,364,627	8	98
1887	4,476,447	13	96
1888	5,590,576	28	94

1889	5,707,061	17	34
1890	5,825,951	16	41
1891	5,713,859	12	32

*the figures are taken from the Report of the Commissioner of Police of the Metropolis for the years 1891. The population count between the census years of 1881 and 1891 were estimates on behalf of the Registrar General.[125]

---

[125] Peter Stubley, *1888 London murders in the year of the Ripper.* (Stroud, the History press, 2012), p. 246.

Chapter Four
Inconvenient People

Dreaded by most, nineteenth-century asylums show a small insight how the Victorians understood and treated the mentally ill. Cures were limited, and good intentions helped no one, these became the home of society's outcasts. Visitors were restricted with various emotions running high to the residents, many stories are told how badly treated people were and fear of the unknown. Asylums were an essential part of Victorian society often called 'an institution shelter for the insane'. Along with the workhouses, cemeteries and harsh boarding schools those words rang fear to Victorian societies.

"Asylums were slowly constructed during the eighteenth century, and all were charitably funded. Bethlem was followed by Bethel in Norwich in 1712-13, and a further nine followed."[126]

There were also strange notions regarding the treatment of the mentally ill. In the Bensham Asylum, for example,

---

[126] Sarah Rutherford, *The Victorian Asylum.* (Oxford, Shire publications 2008), p. 9.

doctors had come to believe that the clean air and healthy situation of the suburbs would help its patients overcome their problems. The doctors believed that people often became insane because they lived in bleak surroundings and did not have enough food to eat. Therefore, asylums were encouraged to provide nutritional food, a moderate quantity of malt liquor, and comfortable, warm bedding. Patients were allowed to exercise and bathe, and were sometimes bled, which was a process of releasing some blood from the body in a controlled way. Of course, there was some mistreatment meted out to the patients by the doctors and some asylums were horrible places. The 1844 Commissioners' Report censured eleven such institutions, including the Wreckenton Lunatic Asylum. According to the report, patients often only had a plain bread and water or milk for breakfast and pea soup for dinner and were frequently restrained. This treatment was extremely unacceptable, and most people were shocked when the report became public. At the beginning of the nineteenth century, there were only eight pauper asylums throughout the British Isles, and their care was paid for by charitable bodies. The rest of the country saw their lunatics being cared for in either the Poor Law Workhouses, or within private 'Madhouses' that were licensed under the 1774 Madhouse Act. This often led to the mistreatment of many lunatics as there was little understanding of their condition and due to over-crowding, it was not uncommon for lunatics to be shackled is these early madhouses. In 1808, the first county asylum act was passed, with a second one being passed in 1845, which made the construction of the Victorian asylum compulsory for all counties.[127] The asylums are depicted in Victorian literature as dark, scary places filled with animalistic, dangerous creatures which makes for a good, thrilling read for both contemporary and modern readers alike. However, whilst researching the history of these asylums, it becomes clear all was not as it appeared. Husbands admitted wives to asylums to be rid of them, some mentally ill women were locked away in domestic households to avoid embarrassment and others were treated as though they were insane because they had a vast imagination which currently would be celebrated, not condemned. Victorian literature was able to tackle the taboo subject of mental illness and experiment with it in stories, covering every angle of the topic. These Victorian ideas on asylums and mental illness are still recognised today, displaying just how powerful and influential they are.

Pauper Lunatic: Unable to pay for care, so confined in a lunatic ward of the local work house, in a county asylum or in a private asylum with fees paid for by the parish out of the local poor rates.

Private Patient: Able to pay fees, or to have fees paid for by family.

Chancery Lunatic: A sub-category of 'private patient', a wealthy private patient who had been found insane by inquisition and whose large estate/income was deemed at risk because of the patient's incapacity to manage his/her affairs, thereby requiring the protection of the Lord Chancellor. Such cases were dealt with by the Masters in lunacy and their conditions were inspected by the Lord Chancellors visitors.

---

[127] *thetimechamber.co.uk/beta/sites/asylums*

Criminal Lunatic: Found not guilty of a crime by reason of insanity and confined in Royal Bethlehem hospital, or, later, Broadmoor or Rampton hospitals.

The administration of pauper lunacy also involved co-operation between asylum and Poor Law officials. In the study, The Poor Law of Lunacy, Peter Bartlett steers away from the traditional history of confinement set in the context of the rise of the medical profession and the power exerted by alienists. He convincingly argues that county asylums were Poor Law institutions that should be understood in the context of the nineteenth-century Poor Law. His analysis of the administrative structures involved in the construction and operation of county asylums shows that 'asylum doctors had little role in deciding how asylum construction would occur, and who would be placed in or removed from county asylums'. Poor Law officials and Justices of the Peace were charged with making decisions about the construction of asylums, and who was to be admitted and discharged. Under the 1834 Poor Law Amendment Act, Poor Law relieving officers were made responsible for organising the applications for admission to the local asylum.[128] After 1853, Poor Law Medical Officers were given the authority to sign the statutory medical certificate required for the admission of pauper lunatics. Bartlett contrasts this with the asylum medical superintendent who played no role in admission and patient certification. Despite being the medical professional and lunacy expert, he was exempt from signing medical

---

[128] P. Bartlett, *The Poor Law of Lunacy. The Administration of Pauper Lunatics in Mid Nineteenth Century England* (London, 1999), p.2.

certificates and admitted patients based on an outsider's authority. Justices of the Peace and Poor Law officials effectively controlled the admission process which, in Bartlett's opinion, made county asylums "an institution legally based in the Poor Law". Bartlett concludes that it "was only with the introduction of the Poor Law relieving officers and medical officers that the intensive administrative provisions of the Asylum Acts became remotely realisable, and the asylum system could flourish."[129]

The Females: According to case notes, most women came in for short periods only simply to recover from the stress and exhaustion of their domestic lives – once rested and relaxed they were sent on their way. Women were also admitted from problematic marriages or because of giving birth to illegitimate children – even if a result of rape. Post-natal depression was also a common reason for a woman admittance. The female's wards differed vastly from the male wards; they were based around Victorian ideals of femininity with little opportunity for them to go outside and even fewer opportunities to play games. It was only later that this changed, as the attitudes of the country changed. As with the tradition at the time the women's activities were confined to the indoors, which led to a strong bond being formed between both female patients and staff. Furthermore, the women were put to work throughout the asylum, mainly undertaking jobs in the needle room, the laundry and general housekeeping duties around the ward – the latter was kept for problematic patients. The daily routine of the ward remained unchanged

---

[129] Bartlett, *'The Asylum and the Poor Law: The Productive Alliance', p.51.*

for many years, patients would rise at 7 a.m. for breakfast which would consist of coffee, tea or cocoa with porridge and bread as the main course. After breakfast the 'good' patients would have been taken to their respective jobs in the laundry or needle room. Other patients would have waited around until the airing courts were opened later in the morning. Lunch would have been served at around 12:30 and would have consisted of food produced on the local farm; this was their main meal of the day. The airing courts were then opened again in the middle of the afternoon for just over an hour. Tea was served in the early evening and was known to consist of bread and cake. Due to staff shortages on the female side of the hospitals, nurses were known to have dosed the patients with paraldehyde in the evenings to ease the load.

The Males: Most male patients within the asylum system before the First World War were often poor and without spouses to look after them. After WWI, 'shell shock' was a prevalent condition among men admitted to the asylums. At the time of this condition being diagnosed and recognised, it caused controversy due to the condition being like the female psychosis. Alcoholism and the delusion related with it were also common reasons for certification. Unlike the female sides of the asylums, the male sides were smaller in numbers. Escape was more common with male patients than females; due to the smaller numbers of males in some hospitals it was noted that they had a more stable time within the ward. The male's wards had the same daily schedule as the female wards and instead of being involved with the laundry and needle rooms, they worked the kitchen and the bake house. They were also involved in the daily housekeeping of the wards. Other than the difference in activities the male wards were normally run with a stricter discipline; which most of the patients would have been used to give their backgrounds within the military. The male population of the asylums received a wider range of activities for their recovery; they were allowed to join sports teams and the hospital band (if there was one); there were also inter-hospital leagues for them to compete in. Rational patients were also employed on working the farms and the upkeep of the grounds and gardens; they were also employed in various workshops and engineering practices. One such example is an account from an asylum where several male patients were used to lay 2-inch piping to the cricket ground and build a band stand.

Treatments used: The treatments used throughout the history of the asylums have varied massively. When the asylums first opened, there was little knowledge of the psychiatric conditions or how to treat them. Consequently, the lunatics were kept calm and occupied as much as possible, and when the need arouse then restraint was employed. It took many years to begin to understand and develop psychiatric treatments and the first therapy that was employed throughout the asylum system was the treatment of general paralysis of the insane, caused by syphilis, with malaria infected mosquitoes. This treatment was used through until the 1950s when a new drug was developed. The next treatment that was developed was the deep insulin therapy, where it was believed that schizophrenia was caused by a high blood sugar in the brain. Insulin would be administered until the body went into shock and then the patient was revived with a sugary dose of tea. In the 1930s, two major treatments were developed in Europe, these were the electroconvulsive therapy (ECT) and the lobotomy. Both these treatments involved stresses to the brain. ECT involved passing a current through the brain and induce an epileptic fit. This was sometimes known to cause injury to the patient through the severe convulsions. ECT proved to be very effective for patients suffering with depression and still used in very rare cases today. The lobotomy involved cutting the brain tissue within the frontal lobes of the brain. This had mixed results and was discontinued in the 50s. The big breakthrough in the psychiatric treatments was the introduction of drugs to the asylum system. The first drug to be used, discovered by a French naval surgeon was chlorpromazine (laragia) and was the first antipsychotic to be developed and it had a huge impact on the condition of patients. This development led to the rapid introduction of drugs within the psychiatric world. The next large development was talking through patient's problems with them, and occupational therapy. Before the advent of drugs and other treatments, manic, aggressive and suicidal patients were dealt with through restraint. Padded cells were also used to house patients who were self-harming, or violent towards other (see our padded cell section). The most common restraints were the 'straitjacket' and fingerless gloves. Both inhibited the movement of the patient. Less common forms were the use of continuous baths, this is where patients were placed in a warm bath and a sheet affixed over the top with their head and shoulders coming through it. Bed restraints were also used. In the early years of the asylums, restraints were commonplace, and their used recorded. After the 1890 Act, the use of restraints was severely limited and had to be approved by a medical officer and each use recorded.[130]

Self-harm remains a common symptom of mental distress, especially in young women. These days, medication and therapy can relieve painful feelings. But chillingly, notes of a Lady Eliza ends with her being transferred a few months later to the Incurables Department. Emma Riches, a 27-year-old mother of four, fared better. Her newest baby was four weeks old when Emma was admitted to Bethlem with 'puerperal insanity', or what we would now call postnatal depression. She had suffered from the illness after the births of each of the children and been admitted to the same hospital before. Emma wears a 'strong dress', a form of canvas shift that could not be torn by distressed patients. Her record notes: 'She never speaks nor appears to notice anything... She cares for nothing, will not eat unless she is forced to do so, nor dress nor undress herself.' There is no clear indication of how Emma was treated by doctors, beyond a remark that the drugs they tried were ineffectual. Nurses are likely to have attempted to persuade her to sew or help in the kitchens. Uneducated, Emma could not have read books to pass the time or provide an escape from the tedium of the asylum – where she would have been without all her four children. Eventually she is restored to her health, wearing her own smart clothes again and about to be discharged back to her family. After almost a year in hospital, her postnatal depression had passed. Sarah Gardner, a 26-year-old servant from London, felt worthless and wanted to kill herself but was

---

[130]   thetimechamber.co.uk/beta/sites/asylums/asylum-history/the-history-of-the-asylum.

ashamed of her suicidal feelings when admitted to Bethlem. She had been much distressed by the social stigma and gossip about her situation as a single woman working for a man. She'd also been jilted by her fiancé. She stayed for only a couple of months before being discharged and 'cured'. Women were thought to be at risk of mental illness caused by supposed disorders of the reproductive system. Cases of melancholia associated with the menopause were treated with leeches to the pubis. The male doctors of the day saw 'hysteria' – from the Latin word for womb – everywhere; almost any form of behaviour, such as excited chattering with other women, could be diagnosed as hysteria. Mercury, known as calomel, was considered an effective treatment for hysteria but, like most of the medicines prescribed for mental illness, was highly toxic. Antimony, a toxic chemical now used in fire retardants, was employed to keep patients in a state of nausea, making acts of violence less likely. It was an early example of the 'chemical cosh'. Women's sexuality was a prime focus of male Victorian physicians. Erotomania (hyper-sexuality) was considered a constant danger in female patients and could accompany hysteria. Physician Thomas Laycock noted that 'the cold bath, the shower bath, the douche and cold applications to the regions of the uterus have all been employed with advantage'. Patients' blood needed cooling and thinning. 'Cerebral congestion', deduced from unusual or manic behaviour, was treated by leeches to the temples, perhaps followed by cold lotions to the shaven scalp. Cold showers were used to cool overheated and overstimulated brains. French physician Jean-Etienne Esquirol recorded subjecting a young woman to a 15-minute cold shower, "after which a shivering came on, her jaws chattered violently, her limbs were unable to support the weight of her body, and the pulse was small, slow and contracted. On waking, reason had returned," he pronounced.[131]

Mental Illness and Asylums of the Victorian Era Asylums and Treatments of Mental Illness from 1837-1901 Mental Asylums Prior To 1850

Before the mid-1800s it was common belief that people with mental illnesses were tainted by the devil. Patients were treated poorly and dwelled in unsanitary conditions. For example, most patients lived in cages, and were given minimal amounts of food; most of the time spoiled or unclean. Patients were treated like animals by their caretakers and facilitators, many of whom believed that the patients were deserving of such inhumanity.

Mental Asylums Post 1850

As science progressed, a movement reform challenged the original beliefs people had about mental illnesses. People began to understand that the mental illnesses were diseases of the brain. They realised that the mentally ill could be cured of their disease. This realisation led to better and more ethical treatments of patients in the asylums. The new discovery fuelled the scientific development in the field. Facilities of the asylum, the introduction of asylums brought relief to the mentally ill committed to jails or those who were abandoned. In the later years, the security of the asylums was unlike

---

[131] www.dailymail.co.uk/home/you/article-2141741/Sent-asylum-The-Victorian-womenlocked-suffering-stress-post-natal-depression-anxiety.html

today; patients could roam free as they were perceived as neither a very big threat nor capable of endangering themselves and were able to go into town. However, in the earlier years patients were kept locked up, with very little privacy in close quarters with others. To pass time, games such as sports and other various recreations were allowed within asylums. As a form of rehabilitation, patients were permitted to work in the facilities such as the kitchen, farms and laundry room. Household chores such as cleaning were performed by the more mentally stable patients. Practices used for treatments such treatments as the rotary chair, solitary confinement and even the electric chair were common practices. The electric chair worked in some cases where the patient was suffering from depression. The rotary chair was presented as more of an experimental treatment as it had no scientific evidence behind the reasoning. Solitary confinement was used only for the violent and suicidal patients; the patients were placed in white padded rooms to prevent them from hurting themselves and other patients. Many of these practices only furthered along the insanity of the inmates. These practices may seem unethical in today's terms, but they were common practice back in the 1800s. A comparison between genders the Victorian asylum was a very gender divided operation and the two sexes were split up. Generally, the men's division was treated better than the women's; in some asylums' cases, the women were permitted to sleep in stables attached to the facility in unsanitary conditions. Women were also understood to not be as mentally stable as men because it was believed that they contained a lesser mental capacity. Women were expected to maintain a passive, withdrawn housewife attitude as too much mental activity such as schooling would improve her chances of developing sanity imperfections. Other groups, such as spinsters and lesbians, were concerning to society because of their alternative life choices and were therefore labelled as mentally unstable and sometimes even a threat. The belief was that not enough male interaction would cause side effects bordering on insanity. Treatment for schizophrenia during the Victorian era, there was little to no understanding at all about schizophrenia. Scientific theories on causes and cures for schizophrenia were surfacing as opposed to the 15th century beliefs on witchcraft and demon possession. Although people recognised schizophrenia as a curable disease, most of the theories were still inaccurate and much of the time caused harm to the patients instead of helping them. Some examples of the early ideas of schizophrenia treatment included: giving patients doses of insulin until they retreated into a state of shock. The patients were then given cups of sugary tea to revive them. Doctors would go about this procedure due to their hypothesis on schizophrenia being caused by high/low blood sugar. Other theories included schizophrenia being caused by circulatory problems. Doctors thought that by letting out blood through leeching and slowing down the amount of blood flowing to the brain, people with schizophrenia would gradually become sane again. Drilling holes in the scull to let out demonic spirits and shock treatment were also used. Rockwood Insane Asylum Kingston, Ontario in the 1850s, when local prisons and penitentiaries as well as families became intolerant of the mentally ill, Rockwood Asylum was established to accommodate these people. Originally, the asylum was intended to house the criminally insane; it soon developed into a 'public' asylum. Although the asylums intended use was a rehabilitation centre for the insane, most of the caretakers within the asylum focused solely on calming the patients rather than helping them to recover. Calming the patients usually lessened the load of work a certain staff member may have.[132] The nineteenth century public asylum was intended to provide therapeutic intervention and safe custody for persons afflicted with insanity. This broadly defined policy was applicable to all patients within the asylum's homogeneous population. However, the balance with which therapy and control were enforced varied between patient categories.[133]

Conclusion

Women in the nineteenth century lived in an age characterised by gender inequality. At the beginning of the century, women enjoyed few of the legal, social or political rights that are now taken for granted in western countries: they could not vote, could not sue or be sued, could not testify in court, had extremely limited control over personal property after marriage, were rarely granted legal custody of their children in cases of divorce, and were barred from institutions

---

[132] https://prezi.com/r2bguokfl0u2/asylums-and-treatments-of-mental-illness-in-thevictorian-era/

[133] SARAH HAYLEY YORK, SUICIDE, LUNACY AND THE ASYLUM IN NINETEENTH-CENTURY ENGLAND. A thesis submitted to The University of Birmingham for the degree of DOCTOR OF PHILOSOPHY, The History of Medicine Unit School of Health and Population Sciences (The University of Birmingham December 2009)

of higher education. Women were expected to remain subservient to their fathers and husbands. Their occupational choices were also extremely limited. Middle and upper class women generally remained home, caring for their children and running the household. Lower-class women often did work outside the home, but usually as poorly-paid domestic servants or labourers in factories and mills. The onset of industrialisation, urbanisation, as well as the growth of the market economy, the middle class, and life expectancies transformed European and American societies and family life. For most of the eighteenth century through the first few decades of the nineteenth century, families worked together, dividing farming duties or work in small-scale family-owned businesses to support themselves. With the rapid mercantile growth, big business, and migration to larger cities after 1830, however, the family home as the centre of economic production was gradually replaced with workers who earned their living outside the home. In most instances, men were the primary 'breadwinners' and women were expected to stay at home to raise children, to clean, to cook, and to provide a haven for returning husbands. Most scholars agree that the Victorian Age was a time of escalating gender polarisation as women were expected to adhere to a rigidly defined sphere of domestic and moral duties, restrictions that women increasingly resisted in the last two-thirds of the century.[134] In a world where patriarchal society enveloped, woman in her circumspect role as daughter, wife and mother, little space

---

[134] Feminism in Literature – Introduction Feminism in Literature Ed. Jessica Bomarito, Jeffrey W. Hunter. Vol. 2. Gale Cengage 2005 eNotes.com 14 Jul 2018.

was allocated to the sexualised female. In contrast, the complex issue of the fallen woman and prostitute occupies much of the art, literature and social reform, constituting an alternative representation within the ideology. Time and time again, a woman's sexual lapse is blamed upon poverty or male seduction. The pre-Raphaelite obsession with restoring the innocence of the fallen woman produced work such as *The Woodman's Daughter* by Millais. Contemporary anxieties surrounding *The Great Social Evil*, therefore, are negated as both the prostitute and fallen female lose all their dangerous independence. Although artistic attempts at disempowering the woman were frequent, Siddall's *Pippa Passing Close to Lose Women* and Egg's *Past and Present* overtly challenge this ideal. The unsavoury topic of desire is foregrounded as the fallen female breaks free from her passive stereotype. Why the woman fell is rarely straightforward; her representation is often manipulated to appease and empower the male spectator.

No doubt the Victorian imagination isolated the fallen woman a so pitilessly from a social context, preferring to imagine her as destitute and drowned prostitute or errant wife cast beyond the human community, because of her uneasy implications for wives who stayed home. In the later nineteenth century, things for women began to change. This undoubtedly had something to do with modernity and its intrinsic insistence on change, clearly it had something to do with the actions of women themselves, with their desire to break out of the limits imposed on their sex. The nineteenth century therefore appears to have been a turning point in the long history of women. The old tensions were still present between work (at home or in the shop) and family, between the domestic ideal and social utility, between the world of appearances, dress, and pleasure and the world of subsistence, apprenticeship, and the practice of a profession, and between religious practice as spiritual exercise and social regulator and the new realm of education in secular schools. Before and at the beginning of nineteenth century, a model of femininity was the 'perfect lady', which was inherited as a Victorian ideal of women. Family and morality were the base of Victorian society, and girls were all taught to submit to the authority and matrimony. The concept of *The Angel in the House*, which was referred to the embodiment of Victorian women, was prevail in the Victorian society. As a result, women in Victorian Age were regarded as incompatible and excluded in many professions. Showalter points out that the first professional activities of Victorian women are either in the home or in womanhood. From the nineteenth century, however, the prevalence of education attributed to the gradual rising incidence of working women. Besides, by the struggles of individuals and feminists, the obstacles to the entry into professions for women, whose exclusion and incompatibility in work had been debated, were removed in the beginning of twentieth century. Meanwhile, the concept of morality and family was strongly suspected by the critics and feminists, who argue that there is no *The Angel in the House*. Within a century, not only female social roles but also female awareness had been emancipated from restraint, though some conventional notions had remained. Women during the Victorian Era lived in a different world from the present. Differences between classes of women were vast. For a high class and middle class, woman had to be an ideal woman for marriage. However, some middle-class women with no husband or father to be taken care of did work as governesses. For the lower class, women had to work for domestic services facing both mental and physical difficulties with low pay and barely any respect. Women worked hard and struggle to prove themselves in the community. Women in the Victorian Era dedicated their hard work and ultimately led to improved conditions for the women in the future.[135] Studies of crime show that in fact there was a steady decline in the number of men, women and children being indicted throughout the nineteenth century, and there is broad agreement among scholars that this flowed from the decline in criminality around the end of the eighteenth century.

There was a sharp (43 per cent) decline in trials for indictable offences between 1860 and 1900. Although the overall trend was down, there were individual years throughout the century in which larger numbers were charged with all varieties of crime – from theft through to murder. The decline in crime has been linked to a range of factors: social order, self-policing within neighbourhoods and communities, the establishment of the police force and the 'civilising' of society, the working class. The increasing economic and political strength of the middle class as they became leaders of society following the upheavals of the Industrial Revolution led to a move towards more restricted social, moral and gender mores, whether through campaigning for the abolition of brutal sports, changes in the courtroom or the expansion of the British Empire. Such restrictions were necessary to preserve decency and exalt the virtues of

---

[135] Essays, UK. (November 2013). Women in The Victorian Era History Essay.

femininity, appropriate masculinity and upright citizenship. Indeed, the 'acceptable' behaviour championed by the expanding middle class was considered applicable not only to the working but also to the upper classes. The Victorian period witnessed several changes dealing with crime. There was the establishment of a professionalised police force with the passage of the Metropolitan Police Act in 1829, which replaced the haphazard system of part-time constables, Bow Street Runners and Thief Takers. Gaols, which previously had housed offenders only until their trial, became huge institutions in which offenders stayed for a longer term. The object of this was not only to punish the offender but also to rehabilitate them. The narrative of women that offended is littered with cases of illegitimate children, domestic violence, poverty, disadvantage and addiction. Even the coolest academic analysis probably, deep beneath the surface, had moments where sympathy or empathy clouded the bigger picture. Occasionally a single piece of paper can return us poignantly and instantly to the people in our histories. A few words scratched in ink help us to remember that even for those how have left little behind there were whole lives full of complex friendships and chances taken or lost. A few lines have the power to transmit feelings of sympathy, sorrow, and hope across centuries. Writing about a criminal woman and brief nineteenth crimes has been a fun opportunity to jump back into the world of female offending, and a great reminder of just how rich and varied the lives, crimes, and stories of these women can be. With so many vivid cases to pick from, it's impossible to pick one that represents the breadth of experiences we trace. Yet, something many of our cases have in common is the ability to challenge our assumptions about the origins and trajectories of wayward women, and to prove just what remarkable histories lie waiting when we follow the right paper trail.

Bibliography

Geoffroy Abbott, *Female executions; Martyrs, murderesses and madwoman*. (Chichester, Summerdale Publishers Ltd, 2013).

Gray, D. (2011*) Contextualising the Ripper murders: poverty, crime and unrest in the East End of London, 1888. Invited Keynote presented to: Jack the Ripper through a Wider Lens: An Interdisciplinary Conference, Bossone Research Enterprise Centre, Drexel University, Philadelphia, USA,* 28-29 October 2011.

H. Allen, *Justice unbalanced*. (Open university press, 1987).

Nina Auerbach, *Woman and the Demon: The Life of a Victorian Myth. (*Boston: Harvard University Press, 1982).

A. Ballinger, *Dead Women Walking: executed woman in*

England and wales, 1900-1955. (Ashgate, Dartmouth 2000).

P. Bartlett, *The Poor Law of Lunacy. The Administration of Pauper Lunatics in Mid-Nineteenth Century England* (London, 1999),

J. M. Beattie, *'The criminality of women in eighteenth-century England', Journal of Social History, 8* (1975).

Neil R. A. Bell, Trevor N Bond, Kate Clarke and M W. Oldridge. *The A-Z of Victorian Crime.* (Stroud, Amberley Publishing, 2016).

Charlotte Beyer, *True Crime and Baby Farming: Representing Amelia Dyer. (2015).*

Feminism in Literature – Introduction Feminism in Literature Ed. Jessica Bomarito, Jeffrey W. Hunter. Vol. 2. Gale Cengage 2005 eNotes.com 14 Jul 2018.

S. Webb & M. Brown. *Mary Ann Cotton: Victorian Serial Killer*, (Durham, The Langley Press 2016).

Judith Butler, *Gender Trouble.* (New York, Routledge, Chapman and Hall Inc., 1990).

Frances E. Dolan, *Dangerous Familiars: Representations of Domestic Crime in England, 15501700* (London: Cornell University Press, 1994).

Kelly Grovier, *The Gaol; the story of Newgate prison, London's most notorious Prison.* (London, a Hachette UK Company, 2009).

Dorothy L. Haller, *Bastardy and Baby-farming in Victorian England.* This paper was selected by the Department of History as the Outstanding Paper for the 1989-1990 academic year.

Donald Haase, *The Greenwood Encyclopaedia of Folktales and Fairy Tale,* (Westport, CT: Greenwood Press, 2008).

Louise Jackson, *Child Sexual Abuse in Victorian England.* (London: Routledge, 2000).

Yvonne Jewkes, *Media and Crime.* (Sage Publications, 2010).

Dr Peter Joyce, *Criminology, A complete introduction.* (Great Britain, Hodder & Stoughton. 2012).

Jenny Kennode and Gailbine Walker, *Women, Crime and the Courts in Early Modern England*, (UCL Press Ltd., 1994).

Anne-Marie Kilday, *Women and Violent Crime in Enlightenment Scotland* (Woodbridge: Boydell Press, 2007).

P. King, *'Female Offenders, Work and Life-Cycle in Late Eighteenth-century London', Continuity and Change, 11,* (1996).

Claudia C. Klaver, Rosenma and Ellen Bayuk, *Other Mothers: Beyond the Maternal Ideal.* (Columbus: Ohio State University press 2008).

A. Lloyd, *Doubly Deviant Doubly Damned, society's treatment of violent women.* (1995).

Andrew Maunder and Grace Moore. *'Introduction.' Victorian Crime, Madness and Sensation.* (Hampshire and Burlington: Ashgate, 2004),

Kristen R. Neville, *The insanity defence: A comparative analysis.* (Eastern Michigan University, 2010). Senior Honours Theses. 244. http://commons.emich.edu/honors/244.

Chris Payne. *The* Chieftain*: Victorian True Crime through the Eyes of a Scotland Yard Detective.* (Stroud: The History Press, 2011),

J. Purvis, *Women's History: Britain, 1850-1945: An Introduction.* (New York, UCL press, 1995),

Denise Riley, *'Am I That Name?' Feminism and the Category of 'women' in History,* (Macmillan, 1988).

Fiona Rule, *Worst Street in London.* (Surrey, Allan Publishing Ltd, 2008),

Sarah Rutherford, *The Victorian Asylum.* (Oxford, Shire publications 2008),

Reginald Scot, *'The Discoveries of Witchcraft'*, (London, 1584), as cited in *Walker, Crime, Gender and Social Order*,

J. Wallach Scott, *Gender and the Politics of History*, (Columbia University Press, 1988).

J. A. Sharpe, *'Domestic homicide in early modern England', The Historical Journal,* 24 (1981).

Radojka Start-up, Damaging Females: Representations of women as victims and perpetrators of crime in the mid nineteenth century. (Submitted for the degree of Doctor of Philosophy to the Department of History, University College London, February 2000).

Neil. R Storey, *The Victorian Criminal.* (Oxford, Shire Publications Ltd, 2011).

Peter Stubley, *1888 London murders in the year of the Ripper.* (Stroud, the History press,2012),

David, J, Vaughan. *Mad or Bad, Crime and insanity in Victorian Britain.* (Barnsley, Pen and Sward Ltd, 2017).

Garthine Walker, *Crime, Gender and Social Order in Early Modern* England, in Kermode and Walker (eds.), *Women, Crime and the Courts.* (Cambridge: Cambridge University Press, 2003).

Judith Walkowitz, *Prostitution and Victorian Society: Women, Class and the State,* (Cambridge, Cambridge University Press, 1980).

Nigel Wier, *British Serial Killers.* (Bloomington, IN: Author House, 2011).

Lucy Williams, *Wayward Woman. (*Barnsley, Pen & Sward books Ltd, 2016).

Anthony S. Wohl, *Endangered Lives, public health in Victorian Britain*. (Cambridge, Cambridge University press, 1983).

Primary Sources

Berkshire Chronicle, 18 April 1896. Viewed 27/02/2017.
The Watford Observer, (seen 25/04/2018).

Auckland Times and Herald 27th March 1873.

Old Bailey proceedings online, (
https://www.oldbaileyonline.org/browse.jsp?id=t189605184
51&div=t18960518-451&terms=amelia_dyer#highlight)
18th May 1896, trial of Amelia
Elizabeth Dyer, (REF: t18960518-451).

Old Bailey proceedings online, (
https://www.oldbaileyonline.org/browse.jsp?id=t189605184
51&div=t18960518-451&terms=amelia_dyer#highlight)
18th May 1896, trial of Amelia Elizabeth Dyer, (REF:
t18960518-451).

Report of the commissioner of police of the metropolis for the
year 1888, p. 27

The National Archives:

(TNA) crim 1/44/10

(TNA) Mepol. 3/95

(TNA) Pri. Com. 8/44

(TNA) A 5/858/31a

(TNA) A5/ 858/30

(TNA) A5/858/28

Websites

http://historybytheyard.co.uk/baby_farming.htm

*http://www.todayifoundout.com/index.php/2015/06/garrottin
g-panic-1850-insane-wayspublic-reacted/.*

*http://www.todayifoundout.com/index.php/2015/06/garrottin
g-panic-1850-insane-wayspublic-reacted/.*

panic-1850-insaneways-public reacted/.

*https://www.historic-
uk.com/HistoryMagazine/DestinationsUK/Newgate-Prison-
Wall/.*

*https://www.historic-
uk.com/HistoryMagazine/DestinationsUK/Newgate-Prison-
Wall/.*

www.bbc.co.uk/history/british/victorians/crime_01.shtml.
thetimechamber.co.uk/beta/sites/asylums.

https://prezi.com/r2bguokfl0u2/asylums-and-treatments-of-mental-illness-in-thevictorian-era/.

Appendices

Plate 1

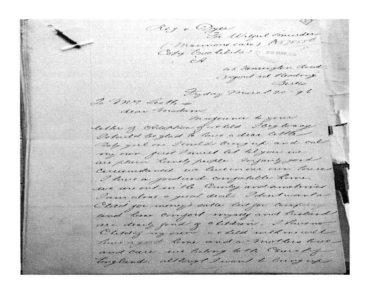

Plate 2

the Child as my own I should not
mind the Mother or any friend coming
to see the Child any time. It would
be a satisfaction to see and know the
Child was going on all right. Only
hope we may come to terms. I should
like to have Baby as soon as you
can arrange it. If I could come for
her I dont mind paying my fees one
way. I should break my journey at
Gloucester. I have a friend in the
Asylum. I should be glad to call and
see. Kindly let me have a early reply
I can give you good reference and
any other particular you may ask
me. I shall be pleased to answer.
        I am yours Respectfully
            A Harding

enclosed in the above letter was a
piece of paper with the following written
on.
        Mrs Harding
        115 Kensington Road
            Oxford road
                Reading Berks

88

Plate 3

115 Kensington rd.
Oxford rd Reading
—Sunday March 22. 96

To Mrs Roll,

Dear Madam many thanks
for your letter of this morning. I shall
not answer anyone else until I hear
from you again. I do hope we may
come to terms, rest assured I will do
my duty & that dear child. I will be
a Mother as far as possible be in
my power and if I come for her of
you like to come and stay a few
days or a week later on I shall be
pleased to make you welcome. It is
just lovely here. In the summer there
is a orchard opposite our front door,
you will say it is healthy and pleasant.
Hoping to hear soon

I am yours
CA Harding

Ethel Lorris a very pretty name
I am sure she ought to be a pretty child

Plate 4

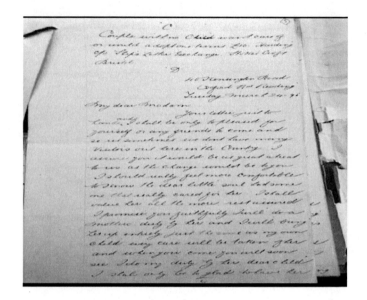

Plate 5

Plate 6

n the   18 .

Records respecting the Executioner and his Assistants (if any).

Name and Address, in full, of the Executioner.	Name and Address, in full, of the 1st Assistant to the Executioner (if any).
James Billington. Market Street Farnworth. nr. Bolton.	Wm Wilkinson. 9 East Bank S. Bolton

d Medical Officer as to the manner in which each of the
has performed his duty.

1. Yes.	1. Yes.

Plate 7

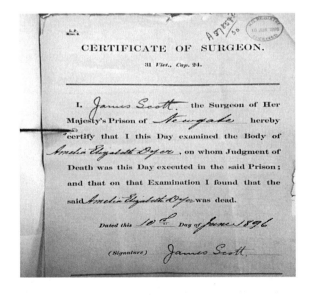

CERTIFICATE OF SURGEON.

31 *Vict.*, *Cap.* 24.

I, James Scott, the Surgeon of Her Majesty's Prison of Newgate hereby certify that I this Day examined the Body of Amelia Elizabeth Dyer, on whom Judgment of Death was this Day executed in the said Prison; and that on that Examination I found that the said Amelia Elizabeth Dyer was dead.

Dated this 10th Day of June 1896

(Signature) James Scott.

Plate 8

H.M. Prison. *Newgate*

June 10 1896.

GENTLEMEN,

As directed in paragraph 9 of Standing Order, No. 225, I have the honour to submit the annexed Record of the execution of prisoner

Amelia Elizabeth Dyer

which took place at *Nine* o'clock on the morning of the *10th instant*.

The Inquest was held on the same day.

The jury returned the following verdict :—*

Death by Hanging.

The execution passed off satisfactorily.

Your obedt Servant

E S Milman

Governor

To the Prison Commissioners.

* A note should be added of any observations of the jury, or other matters of importance which arose during the inquest.